Devil Girls of Ancient Rome

and the men who loved them

Jacob Rabinowitz

Contents

Preface: Fossils of Lust..9

Catullus

The Colonia Bridge..13
Camerius' Friend..15
The Door..16
Aemilius..18
Ipsitilla..19
Flavius 20
Time...22
The Sparrow...23
The Stars..24
Death of a Sparrow...25
Tavern of Fuckers...26
Egnatius...27
Rufus..29
Rufa...30
The Flower..31
Furius..32
You Know You Love It..33
Ariadne..34
Berenice...41
Attis..46

5

Tibullus' Priapic Poem..53

Cerberus
A Triple Homage to Sextus Propertius

A Psychic Geography of Masochism.....................................59
The Case of Propertius..69
Selected Poems of Propertius:
    Mental Illness...75
    Ariadne...78
    Battle..81
    Ghosts..83
    The Rout..89

The Rotting Goddess

Dedication...97
Introduction...99

Part One: Hecate

She is a Tree of Life..103
Queen of Heaven, Queen of Hell.......................................123
Underneath the Moon..137
A Howling at the Gate..147

Part Two: The Witch

Descent of the Goddess...159

Nigra Sum Sed Formosa...169

The Witch of Endor...189

Into the Cauldron...195

Conclusion...205

Fossils of Lust

My mother was a psychiatrist, and there were all sorts of interesting books on the shelves in my home. One of my earliest childhood memories is reading Richard Freiherr von Krafft-Ebing's *Psychopathia Sexualis* and trying to make out the Latin phrases. These were employed like a sort of classical fig-leaf, to reserve the more poignant details for the qualified eyes of physicians and psychologists. I still recall the sense of triumph with which I returned from my first year at college, having read Cicero and Ovid, and retrieved my old favorite. What an edifying evening I spent deciphering the naughty oracles sown throughout the volume like raisins in the bread of knowledge!

The classics have always had an amusingly lurid undertone. The very idea of Latin and Greek evokes the splendors of English public schools, where boys acquired the skills to administer a colonial empire through bare-bottom whipping, furtive homosexual sex, and the close study of carefully expurgated editions of the classics.

And those who are old enough to remember brick-and-mortar second-hand bookstores, will recall the slightly sequestered section labeled CURIOSA, where one found elegant limited editions of *The Satyricon* and histories of the more vicious Caesars, with edifying illustrations.

Antiquity has its piquant side, and this is what really drew us to the classics — at least those who were any good at it. This volume recollects some less glimpsed vistas from that happy past. My undertaking here is an archaeology of desire, a paleography of dreams. As William S. Burroughs wrote in the preface for the original edition of my Catullus translation,

Frivolous. Trivial. Profound. Obscene. Dead fingers talk in Braille. Read the fossils of lust.

Catullus

Catullus, one of the earliest Roman poets, dead before he was thirty, wrote all of his extant poetry under the influence of Clodia, the unfaithful wife of a gangster. Catullus refers to her by the literary code-name Lesbia. Catullus' love lyrics to her, have the doomed beauty one associates with Poe or Dowson.

Catullus' other works also echo his passion for powerful, cruel women. His miniature epics all describe doomed relationships and romantic desertions. Catullus writes with greatest conviction, clearly from experience, in the female role. He is the used and abandoned Ariadne, the castrated Attis.

But most memorable, and not least brilliant, are the insult poems; still funny after two thousand. Personally, I have always rated a good laugh over a great truth, or I would have, had I thought there was some important difference. But here the truth, at least the psychological one, is Catullus' jealous anxiety towards his rivals for Clodia. They are all monsters of appetite, and threaten in various ways to *devour* her. If we read aright Catullus' fascinated, hallucinatory exaggerations of the sexual activity of his rivals, we see the obsessive humiliated reveries of the cuckold: strange pleasures confessed from behind the mask of comedy.

The Colonia Bridge

Colonia, I know you want to have a festival procession along
that long bridge of yours. You're all set to go bounding
over it —
but the bridge shakes in apprehension on its bandy-legged
trestles
patched and propped with odd lumber scraps.
It's afraid of falling back-flat into deep swamp.

I personally hope your bridge'll be so good to you it could
even stand up to the priests of Mars
hopping and howling the war-dance all across it.
— In return for these good wishes of mine, I'd like, as a
favor, a good laugh.
Could it be arranged for one of my fellow citizens to slip
from the bridge, sail over the side and head-first under
the mud
at the deepest point in that whole semi-liquid lake
where the rotting marsh achieves its richest shade of oily
blue-black?
The guy's a jerk. He's about as knowing as a two-year-old
asleep in his father's rocking arms.
Now he's married a young girl, a glory of innocent
freshness, a flower,
a girl as dainty-soft as a baby goat,
a girl deserving more painstaking protection than the rich
dark grapes perfecting on the vine.

Yet he lets her play where she pleases, he doesn't care,
    doesn't bestir himself
any more than an axe-hacked hunk of log half sunk in a
    green-mantled standing pool.
The numbskull sees, hears nothing, doesn't know what, or if,
    he is.
So shake him out of that dullness, pitch him off, O bridge;
have him leave his former sluggish life behind in that thick
    slime
as a mule might lose its iron shoe in sucking mud.

Camerius' Friend

Camerius, if it isn't too much trouble, I'd really like to know
    where you're hiding out these days.
I looked for you at the racetrack, the bookstores,
    Jupiter's temple, Pompey's theater —
I stopped all the girls, demanded your whereabouts — they
    denied any knowledge, faces calm with innocence.
I wasn't satisfied. "You tramps," I pressed, "where's
    Camerius? I know you know!"
One of them opened her blouse and said:
"Here he is, hiding between my tits!"
Camerius, old buddy, being your friend is a labor of
    Hercules . . . .

The Door

Catullus:
Door, ever a pleasure to old Balbus, when the house was his,
door, that was always nice to his sweet son Caecilius, now
    just married. Door, Jove bless your every hinge!
Everyone had a good word for the way you opened to
    Balbus
— though the word is you aren't guarding his son very well.
Since the old man was laid to rest and the young heir got
    himself married,
you've really let things slide.
Come on, out with it, what's the story behind your change of
    heart?
why'd you betray your old loyalty?

Door:
As I wish to please Caecilius, who owns me now, I did
    nothing wrong — whatever people say!
But whenever folks are angry, they slam the door!
Whatever's wrong, it's the door's fault!

Catullus:
Could you be a little more explicit?

Door:
Can I? No one wants the trouble of learning about things
    they're already sure they know.

Catullus:
I'm honestly interested. Don't worry, just tell.

Door:

Well, for a start, that "virgin bride" of Caecilius' was already
married once.

Not that her first husband ever touched her — his weak little
prick dangled like a rotten carrot. It never raised its head
belt high.

But they say his father broke into the bedroom (a disgrace to
the whole unhappy house),

either because his wicked brains were stewed with lust, or
because his helpless son couldn't plough his own field

and they had to find a prick that packed enough punch to
relieve the girl of her virginity.

Catullus:

A loyal, staunch, upstanding father — who'd piss in his
own son's lap!

Aemilius

So help me all the gods, I really don't think it makes much
    difference
if you sniff Aemilius' mouth or his ass.
As far as cleanliness goes, they're quite the same.
If anything, his ass is neater, and nicer,
since it has no teeth, whereas his mouth —
well, they're more like tusks
stuck in gums like split wrinkled rawhide,
and when he smiles —
did you ever see, on a summer's day,
the parted cunt lips of a pissing mule?

Aemilius has fucked plenty of girls, he thinks he's really
    sharp —
though at first glance I took him for a not very valuable
    slave,
the sort one employs to drive a donkey that turns a mill

And if any girl could touch him, wouldn't she be the kind
who'd rim a sick executioner?

Ipsitilla

O please, my sweet Ipsitilla, dear delightsome child, let me
    come visit you at noon?
You will? And one other thing — be sure no one else is there.
    Be sure you're at home, leave the door unlocked, get
    ready
for nine uninterrupted fucks. In fact, why not now? I just
    had lunch, I'm lolling here, gorged,
practically punching a hole through my toga.

Flavius

What about your new playmate, Flavius? Unless she's a total
    dog I don't see how you can help telling.
On the other hand, who knows what kind of hot little whore
    turns you on?
One thing's for sure, you're not alone at night. So says the
    cologne you've started using,
and the crumpled blankets on your flattened mattress.
So says your trembling bed, in a squeak, lurching across the
    floor.
Keeping mum can't mask the facts. Look at the bags under
    your eyes
— you're all fucked out!
So come on, tell me who it is.
I want to glorify your exploits
in elegant, heavenly verse.

Lesbia

The next group of poems are addressed to Catullus' great love, Lesbia, and to his rivals for her affections. Lesbia was an older women, sister of a gangster and a consul's wife, whom Cicero once referred to as a "two-bit Lady Macbeth" (in Latin, a quadrantia Clytemnestra).

Her actual name was Clodia. In deference to convention, Catullus spared her reputation by giving her a literary code-name. The name Lesbia refers, of course, to Sappho of Lesbos. To ancient ears the adjective "Lesbian" suggested poetry — which was considered wondrous; not homosexualtity — which was considered ordinary.

Time

The time to live, the time to love, is now. What our parents
    think about it means nothing to us.
It can't wait. Every morning the sun returns to life —
our light is brief as a day, our night is an endless sleep.
Give me a hundred kisses, a thousand, ten thousand, into
    the millions, into infinity,
I've got to lose count, lose myself, lose my distrust.
Give me a hundred kisses, a thousand, ten thousand,
if I haven't lost count I know there aren't enough.

The Sparrow

The Sparrow was, for the ancients, the animal emblem of romantic love. In Greek myth, sparrows drew the chariot of Venus.

Sparrow, my girl's favorite pet, she keeps you in her lap,
    amused at you,
lets you attack her fingertip, provokes your sharp little nip.
She's the shining center, the glowing focus
of my life. It pleases her to toy with you,
sweet thing, the play-bites distract her from every
    sharper pain.

Maybe I could shake this grim feeling I have
if I could play with you as she does — just forget myself and
    play.

The Stars

You want to know how many kisses would be enough for
me, Lesbia?
The number of sand grains between the tombs of Libya's
    ancient lords
and the temples where Egypt worships Jove in the shape of a
    ram.
The number of stars that watch the furtive
love affairs of humankind
while the night is passing over them in silence.
That's how many would satisfy your crazed Catullus,
What can't be counted can't be an unlucky number.

Death of a Sparrow

Venus and Cupid, Spirits of Love,
lament; Desires and Passions, mourn;
and all you warmhearted men-about-town,
weep now, for my girlfriend's sparrow is dead,
her darling bird, more precious to her than sight.
It was sweet, and it knew her
as well as she knew her own mother.

It used to stay right in her lap, hopping
about, here and there, chirping only for its mistress.
Now it goes the black path they say none travel back.

Damn you Death, life's ugly shadow!
You swallow every beautiful thing,
you stole my lovely, delightful bird.
A crime! Poor little sparrow!
My girl's in tears,
her eyes are red and faintly swollen.

Tavern of Fuckers

There's a low dive nine shops down from the temple of
    Castor and Pollux
where a crowd hangs out who think they own the only dicks
    extant,
that they're the only ones allowed to screw girls,
that everyone else is a nerd.

Dimwits! Don't you know I've got enough schlong to gag
    two hundred like you?
Think about it. And afterward I'd scribble your tavern-front
with how I rate you as cocksuckers.

The girl who slipped from my arms
  — I loved her. No one will ever love a girl that much
  — my hard-conquered lady now resorts to this dump.
All you splendid young aristocrats love her, and, I'm sorry
    to say, so do all the grubby little street-corner sultans
    who conduct their amours in alleyways.

But especially you, Egnatius, with your elegantly-cut, long
    fop's hair,
you son of Celtiberia, land famous only for its rabbits,
who, like your barbarian ancestors, believe a thick beard
    makes you lovely,
yes, and teeth that shine from being rinsed in your own piss.

Egnatius

Egnatius always has a smile, his teeth are sparkling   white.

If he's at court to help in a friend's defense,
when the lawyer's making the jury sob,
he grins.

At a funeral, when the groans of the mourners rise with the
    crackling of the pyre,
and the widowed mother cries for her lost, only and
    devoted son
— Egnatius grins.

Whatever the place, whatever the case,
he's got his lips working, the fellow is smirking.
It isn't very nice.
No, and it isn't refined or elegant or smart. It's *sick*.

Therefore, I feel I should warn you:
were you a slick Sabine or a witty Tiburian,
a thrifty Umbrian or a paunchy Etruscan gourmand,
a Lanuvian whose dark skin sets off his smile, a
    Transpadane like my ancestors,
or *anyone* who cleans his teeth decently — I still wouldn't
    wish this continual grinning.
There's nothing so awkward as misplaced mirth.

Now, you're a Celtiberian. It's a well documented fact that in
    the regions of Celtiberia
the custom is to brush the teeth and rub the pink gums with
    one's own morning urine.

Thus, we can only conclude that the shine of your teeth
is an accurate indication of how much piss you've drunk.

Rufus

You really shouldn't be surprised, Rufus, that no woman
    wants to feel your weight upon her,
not even if you corrupt her with new clothes or clear
    delightful gems.
An unpleasant breath of rumor wafts about you like an odor
— to the effect that a wild goat lives in the valley of your
    armpit.

Everyone's a little apprehensive.
A very ugly beast, the goat is,
no fashionable girl would sleep with one.
Therefore, you should either kill that implacable enemy of
    noses,
or stop wondering why ladies run away.

Rufa

Rufa, the carrot-haired girl from Bologna,
gives blow jobs to her little brother,
red-headed Rufus. You know who she is,
Menenius' wife, the one you always see
in the paupers' graveyard, grabbing snacks
from food offerings set on the pyres.
Whenever she chases a loaf rolling out
of the blaze, the unshaven slave who tends
those flames runs over and gives her a whack.

The Flower

Furius and Aurelius, you'd follow your Catullus
    anywhere:
to where the utmost shores of India re-echo the river Ocean
    thrashing its way around the disk of Earth,
to Hyrcania, to silken Arabia, to Scythia's frozen fields,
to the archer Parthian's home, to where the seven mouths of
    Nile shoot silty color into the Mediterranean,
or up the skyish Alps to look out over Gaul, the Rhine, the
    terrifying sea, and Britain out on the world's rim
(now they're mere memoranda of Caesar's conquering).
My friends, ready to adventure so far off with me, taking
    chances on the gods' good will,
I only ask you to ferry back a message, not very long or very
    nice, to my girl:
that I hope she's getting on well with her lovers she takes on
    three hundred at a time,
loving not one, but all the same milking their dicks on an
    assembly-line basis,
not caring about my love — like she used to — my love cut
    down (her fault),
like a flower at the edge of a field razed by the passing
    plough.

The next two poems are directed at Catullus' rivals for the affections of a fourteen year old boy named Juventius.

Furius

Furius owns neither slave nor strongbox, he couldn't host so
    much as a spider or a bedbug, his hearth doesn't house a
    living coal.
But he certainly has a father, and a stepmother whose teeth
    could crunch through flint.

You get on just fine, Furius, with your dad and his dried
    stick of a wife.
No wonder — indigestion's no problem, you've
    nothing to fear from fire,
your roof's not about to cave in, theft is impossible, your
    death would make no inheritors — you're exempt from
    every peril.

Isn't it great? Sun, cold and hunger have given you bodies
    drier than horn.
You're free from sweat, saliva, mucus, phlegm
— and as if that were insufficiently spic-and-span,
your ass is clean as a salt-shaker.
You don't crap ten times in a year,
and when you do, it's harder than a bean or a pebble.
You could crush it in your hands and never stain a finger!
Don't belittle your blessings, Furius, enjoy what you have.
And quit pestering me for that loan — you're already
    fortunate enough.

You Know You Love It

I fuck your asses, I feed you my dick, Aurelius (you love it)
    and cock-sucking Furius.
You said that I lack decency, basing your charge on a few
    little verses about a boy?

Of course a god-fearing poet has to lead an upright life —
    that's no reason his poems shouldn't live it up
— poems which are witty, elegant compositions, even if they
    are a bit unbuttoned,
even if they do scratch you where it always itches, even if
    they do get people steamed up —
I don't mean just schoolboys, no, even big hairy studs, real
    animals, guys who need both hands to lift their dicks.
You thought I was naughty for writing the poem about
    wanting a million kisses?
Well fuck you.

Ariadne

They say Mount Pelion's topmost pines
once swam the great sea's fluent waves
when the chosen, toughest young men of Greece,
hoping they could steal the golden fleece,
dared go the ocean in a quick ship,
raking the dark blue water plains with fir-tree oars.

For them the goddess who holds the Acropolis
hill-topping high Athens
herself invented that water chariot
zooming on the lightest breeze. She assembled
the piney woodwork of the curving keel.
The speed of that first ship was
education to Amphitrite — then still a naive
young brine-goddess.
Pallas built that yacht whose beakish prow
ploughed up the plains of windy sea —
the waters wrenched by oarage foamed white and spit
	glitter.
Suddenly nymphs of the waves raised their faces
clear of the twinkling flood,
surprised by *this* sea-monster.
Then and only then did mortals see by daylight
the daughters of Nereus all naked,
standing up to their breasts in the whirling silver.

Then, they say, Peleus ignited
with love for Thetis, who, for her part,
didn't scorn a mortal marriage. Even her father
judged they should join.

Heroes, born in that most desirable time of all the ages,
my chants will summon up all of you
often, and especially you, uniquely greatened
by the blaze of your wedding torches, all-fortunate Peleus.

Jupiter'd wanted Thetis for himself, but the father of the
        gods
yielded her to you, defender of Thessaly.
Thetis accepted you, Tethys and Oceanus,
who include the whole disk of earth in a fluid embrace,
let you lead their granddaughter away.

The wanted time came, all Thessaly crowded
the house, the palace was choked with partying
glad-faced people holding out gifts. The town of Cierum
was derelict, they evacuated the vale of Tempe,
the homes of Crannon, Larissa's walls:
everyone came to pack Pharsalus.
No farming got done, no curved rakes lopped
the ground clear of low-trailing vines, no bull
pulled gouging plough downfield,
tearing up the soil in clods.
No pruning hook thinned tree-shade,
ploughshares left lying roughened with rust.

But the glorious chambers of Peleus' residence
silver-flashed and gold-glared. Every door opened
on a vista of room after rich room receding
into magnificent distance. Throney chairs
glittered white ivory, goblets splashed reflected light
across altarly tables. Glistening

with royal treasure, the whole house joyed. Amid the seats
was the sacred marriage-couch of the goddess,
shaped and smoothed from Indian tusk,
draped with fabric saturate in richest red
then tapestried over with joltingly skillful
images of heroes.

You could see Ariadne on the shore of Naxos,
in the tideline's watery noise,
staring out after Theseus, who falls away
into a vanish, ferried out of sight
by no slow boat. She stands there, madness
building up inside her, not believing
she's really seeing this — she's just then waking
from her cheating sleep, and starting
to comprehend she's been ditched, left sorrow-sick
on the blank unpeopled sand.

The young man of memory conveniently weak
fled, his oars beating back the waves, his meaningless
promises blown in the storm, words in the wind.

The daughter of royal Minos, standing in the seaweed,
looks out after him with sad sweet eyes,
staring, rigid, looking like that famous
statue of the Bacchante stunned by the god.

The sea-breeze doffs her gauzy turban,
her dress falls delicate down from shoulder,
frees her firm little breasts,
then everything slips from her body, and the waves roll up
    to touch.

Poor girl, Venus made you crazy with nonstop tortures of
      love
ever since Theseus left the sweep of his home shores
and came to a harsh king's Crete.

A godsent plague had made Athens agree
to pay for having killed a Cretan prince.
They sent a yearly gift of boys and girls
to be Minotaur's dinner. Athens' walls narrowed
on the people so sadly harassed.
Then Theseus chanced his own adventurous body
so his friends wouldn't have a monster's belch
for a funeral oration. He pushed off in a light boat
on a gentle wind, came to tyrant Minos's castle.

Fourteen-years-old, perfumey and warm
from her mother's lap, the royal daughter saw him
and her eye-beams lit. Before she could look down
or turn away, Love seared into her
like a branding iron. The damned, the holy
Thief of Hearts, who mingles our anxieties
with joy, made her moan under her breath
and shiver for the yellow-haired stranger.
And she paled like the gleam on gold
when she learned he'd come courting glory or death
from her brother the monster.

Silent prayers and promises rose from her lips to the gods
      like incense
— sweet and useless. Nothing could stop
the hero's and the Minotaur's collision.
And the Minotaur fell, like a wide-branching oak
or a pitch-sweating pine atop Mount Taurus,

twisted back and ripped out in the whoosh
of a storm wind spinning insane;
all its wooden roots yanked from the ground,
it crashes headlong, busting up forest
and snapping off boughs far around. Thus Theseus
decked that bullbrowed psychopath, beat
that huge brutal body down, goring
only air with its horns. The hero turned back,
big with glory, through the Labyrinth's
mixed-up paths unerrored on the trail of thread he'd left.

Then Ariadne shipped with him to Naxos'
wave-sprayed shore, but he did a quick dissolve as soon as
    sleep put out her lights.
Many times in heart's madness she emptied her chest
in clear loud calls and cries. She climbed
the steep rough mountains to plunge her gaze
over the open sea's flowing tremendous desert,
then she ran down and right out into it,
holding up her fine soft skirts. The slapping waves softly
burst brine against her knees. Wetfaced with tears,
gasping out cold sobs, she told it,

"You took me away from my father, my house,
the altars of my gods, just so you could lose me
on the first empty shore? I believed your fawning voice,
I doomed my brother by helping you.

Did a lioness in labor drop you in the desert?
Did the sea spit you out? Did you swim up into
    existence
from a pool of quicksand? This is how you pay back
the rescue of your life?

At least you could have let me trail after you!
I'd have been a happy slave to wash your feet,
only to make up your purple-quilted bed.

Now you're out in mid-ocean, I'm on the beachhead of
    nowhere.
I wish you'd never come to Crete, bringing the bull
terrible tribute. I'm oceaned off from everyone.
If I could leave now, *would* I go home —
to be the guest of honor at my brother's funeral?
Maybe follow my lover, now bending his ship's tough oars
against the ocean to get away from me?

Furies, snake-haired punishers of men, bring my pain to
him!"

She said. Jove heard. The universe nodded assent,
disheveling sea, lurching earth, flickering all the stars.
Then Theseus forgot the glad flag he promised his father.
Before yielding Theseus to negotiate winds
on the god-built ship, his royal father said,

"My son, whom I meet for the first time only now when I'm
    already old,
do I have to risk never seeing you again, do you have to try
    this adventure?
My luck and your courage have joined to rob me of you
— my eyes are still hungry for the sight of your face.
I cannot gladly let you go, I'll rub dirt and dust in my hair
    for a mourning
and hang black sails on the boat that takes you from me.

Athena help you butcher the bull! Remember when you see
    the home hills,
show you're safe. Raise white sails."

But Theseus's promise left him like a blown cloud quits a
    mountain-top.
His father looked, saw dark sails, jumped the cliff of
    despair.
Brave Theseus was home for the funeral, the daughter of
    Minos avenged.

But even then Bacchus was coming with Silenus and the
    pack of satyrs,
Bacchus came for you, Ariadne, in love with you!
Running insane, the bacchantes turned heads and
    howled,
waved wands and bloody limbs of cows torn up alive.
Some held in baskets the cult's secret emblems — which the
    uninitiate would love to hear about —
they thumped their drums, blew hoarse buzzing
    trumpets,
raised a delicate jingle of brassy chimes,
while barbarian flutes shrilled sweet horrible tunes . . .

Berenice

Catullus' Latin translation of a lost poem by Callimachus.

The king asked angrily: "Who dares to rob
the gods and mock the monarch?" Terror held
the court in awed if awkward quietude.
"Who snitched the lock of hair my royal wife
Berenice deposited in Venus' shrine
— a thankful offering for my return
from devastating all Assyria?"
Then Conon spoke, the court astrologer:

Conon, who'd considered every light throughout the whole
    tremendous heavens,
what hour each is reborn in the blue, what time it dies from
    sight,
when the sun's white blasts of heat will muffle under eclipse,
why the stars move in obedience to Time, how gentle love
    called the moon down from her skyish ride
to set upon Endymion, the sleepy shepherd boy,

— that heavenly scholar, Conon, spoke, and thus appeased
    the king,

"That lock of hair, once Berenice's, now hangs among the
    stars,
placed there by the gods!"

Meanwhile the sad if stellar bangs lamented in the heavens:

"I am those curls Berenice vowed the gods as she
    outstretched her smooth arms in prayer;

41

when the king, enhanced by marrying her, went off to
    devastate Assyria,
still spattered with the traces of that bloody bedtime scuffle
    in which he carried off the queen's virginity.

Do brides really dread the wedding night, do they really
    want to cheat their parents out of grandsons?
So they irrigate the bed-sheets with their phony tears,
so help me all the gods, their groans are faked.

I learned that from the queen's unending complaints
— how she grudged entrusting her man to battle!
Does she claim it wasn't the empty bed she feared —
she only wept because he was her cousin?

I suppose, Berenice, it was only family feeling that made you
    so grief-weak you couldn't walk or speak?

From the vantage-point of your own head I've seen your
    courage,
from earliest girlhood. I remember (if you don't) how you
    slew
the man you were engaged to, so you could marry this king.
The tragic speeches you made the day he left! By Jupiter,
    how often you wiped your eyes!
What god was it transformed your supposed coldness? What
    other god than Love?

The king left. To ensure his return, you sacrificed a bull
and vowed my fuzzy self to the gods. When he came back,
having added Asia Minor, as far as the Euphrates, to Egypt,
she kept her word and I became a tuft twice removed
    — first to the temple, then wafted to the skies —

Against my will, O queen! I swear it by your head! A curse
    upon me
if I lie. But who withstands metal?
The greatest mountain the sun rises over, Athos itself,
    yielded to steel
when Xerxes cut a ship canal through the isthmus and sent
    his barbarian fleet swimming through the slopes.
When such give way to forged tools, what hope for me who
    am mere filament?
Jupiter! May the whole race of Chalybes perish, that Black
    Sea tribe, to whom it first occurred
to disembowel their mother earth and scrape the ore from
    her ribs of rock,
to make the cruel metals!

My sisters wept for me, cut off from them forever, then
    Emathion,
son of the Dawn, appeared, in the form of an ostrich, raising
    a wind at each nod of his stubby wings
— the servant of Venus — he flew me up the night sky, and
    placed me in Aphrodite's holy lap.
(By luck the Love goddess was vacationing in Egypt at the
    time.)
She, lest the crown of Ariadne shine in the sky without
    competition —
she made me gleam there too, soggy with tears, kidnapped
    from the head of blonde Berenice!
A new constellation among the old, I float over by the great
    bear, Callisto, between the lights of Virgo and bad-
    tempered Leo.
I sink nightly down the skies, leading stupid Boötes — better
    known as the little bear — who can hardly find his way

to the ocean to set. He always gets there late.

Though at night I get to hear the footsteps of gods above me,
    day sinks me in the gray sea again.
Nemesis, let me speak this out unpunished — I don't lack
    reverence for the starry company
I'm forced to keep — but all the same
no coward fear will make me hide the truth, though all the
    stars should sing together, *O, come off it, girl!*
Nothing will prevent me from opening my honest   heart
    like a book, that all may read —
all this superlunary stuff doesn't divert me. It's torture to be
    exiled, forever, I presume,
from the dearest head of all, where I fed deliciously on
    pleasantly fragrant moisturizing shampoos, mild
    cleansers and rich conditioners imparting body, bounce
    and luster!

You girls, whom the long-awaited wedding day has joined,
    by torchlight, to your true soulmates,
don't unbutton, setting forth your sweet little titties, before
    you offer up in my honor an alabaster box full of choicest
    hair-care products,
you chaste obedient maidens! But girls who sleep around —
let dirt drink in their spilt gifts — I reject them!
I don't need any favors from unworthy hearts.
But pure new brides, you have my blessing:
may harmony always modulate the measure of your
    wedded lives!

You, my queen, when you stare at the stars and light lamps
    in honor of Venus —
don't let me dry out up here in the breezy ether,

pour out offerings of pure pomade for my frazzled sake.
Oh! I wish the stars would fall! I want to be hair again! Let
    Aquarius glare by Orion in my place."

Attis

Catullus spent a year in Bythynia (Modern Turkey), the center of Cybele's worship. The details he gives of her cult, particularly the description of its music, are vividly authentic.

A fast-moving cruiser shot over deep seas
carrying Attis from Greece to Asia Minor.
He landed, ran through the Trojan groves
into the forest-shadow-world of the goddess.

Angry madness revved his head like an engine —
it didn't seem real when he struck down with sharp flint
and lopped what hung between his legs.
His whole body weakened, feeling
the last of his manhood drain hot down his legs,
blood-spattering the ground.
Then he-she grabbed the light tambourine that thumps out a
    summons
to your sacred rites, Cybele, Great Mother!
Battering the tight bull-hide with soft fingertips,
it, Attis, shivered, started singing to the others:

"You eunuchs, you priestesses of Cybele,
to the high groves — go! you straying cattle,
Cybele's, the Lady of Mount Dyndymus' herd.
In your hearts already exiled, you couldn't wait to leave,
you followed my lead over violent sea,
you unsexed yourselves,
like me, you made yourselves women
and showed your hatred of women's love.
Dance! Our mistress laughs to see us crazed!

To Cybele, run, run, to the groves of the goddess,
where cymbal screams in a metal voice, drum bellows back,
where heavy Phrygian flute buzzes through its curving
    pipes,
where ivy-crowned Maenads dance,
slavering, snapping in convulsions,
electrifying the holy mysteries with loud shrill howls.
Go mad!" sang Attis, the un-woman.

Their tongues flickered out as they yowled the cry of
    Bacchus,
the smooth drum, hollow, thudding, replied,
rattling cymbals clattered shrill,
the whole chorus ran up Mount Ida, gasping,
chaos on a hundred feet.,Attis with his drum in the lead,
like an untamed bullock running from the yoke,
and the Gallae, the sacred eunuchs, ran after.

When they reached the home of Cybele, exhausted,
they fell asleep, nor even thought of food.
Stupor shut their eyes in sinking weakness,
their madness gentled into peace.
When gold-faced sun turned on its beaming eye,
scanning bright white sky, hard ground, rough sea,
scattering night, sleep ran away
from waking Attis. (The Grace Pasithea,
bride of Sleep, eagerly lifted the drowse-god
into her trembling lap.)

Calm and sensitive, without the speeding
madness now, Attis begins to consider what she's done.
Her clear mind sees where she is, without what,
she runs hysterical back to the shore,

47

eyes dropping tears into sea.

"My country, where I was born, country that gave me life,
I left you like a runaway slave — to come to Ida's
snowy forests of wild animals. I wander among their lairs.

Where's home, where can I look for it?
The moment my madness goes
I find only forest. I lost my country,
possessions, friends, family. I lost the forum,
the wrestling matches, the racetrack, the gym.
My soul keeps asking for all I lost, looking for all that's gone.

I had that noblest beauty — which is male.
As man, as adolescent and as boy
I was the star of the gymnasium,
muscles gleaming with oil, glorious, stared at,
garlands were hung on my house, would-be male lovers
    spent their nights in my doorway
— in the morning I had to step over their sleeping bodies.
Am I now the serving girl of the goddess, one of Cybele's
    slaves?
A maenad, a neuter, a piece of what I was?
Will I have to live on cold snowy Ida,
pass my life under Phrygia's tall pillars,
living with deer and wild boar?

Now I regret, now I feel my wound."

As these words passed Attis' red lips, the goddess heard —
Cybele unyoked her chariot's lions, flickered her whip along
    the sides of the left cow-killing beast,

"Go after him, teach him the madness, make him rave again
        — with fear!
Hunt him back to my grove — he thinks he can leave!
Roar, make the whole place tremble resonant,
go, heavy tail slamming against your own flanks,
red mane slapping thick-muscled neck!"

Menacing Cybele spoke and loosed it,
the eager beast ran roaring off, crushing underbrush,
came to the wet white-foaming shore, saw feeble Attis by the
        ocean-plain
and charged. She ran crazily back into the woods, a serving
        girl
for the rest of her life.

Goddess, great goddess Cybele, Lady of Mount Dyndymus,
may all your madness remain far from me —
inspire others, drive others mad.

Tibullus' Priapic Poem

About Priapus

Priapus, child of Venus and Bacchus, represents a universal idea, the phallic fertility god. This is usually represented in archaic societies as some sort of sacred pole. The figure survives in our world in secularized vestige, as the scarecrow and the garden gnome, its meaning relegated to the religious unconscious.

Under the name Priapus this archetype was anciently worshiped on the coast of what is now Turkey and was then Greece, and there particularly at Lampsacus (modern Lapseki). The people of Lampsacus honored Priapus as their founder and stamped his image on their coinage.

Priapus traveled east in Alexander's train, winning hearts for Hellenism. Alexandria became his metropolitan see, where he was celebrated with poetry and public worship. From there he traveled to Rome where, by Augustus' time, no garden was elegant without him.

Our richest vein of Priapic poetry comes from late Republican and early Imperial Rome (roughly 40 BC to 40 AD). The authors of that time, impatient with the crudity of Rome's own literature, imitated the Hellenistic poetry written in Alexandria, two or three hundred years previously, by Callimachus, Apollonius of Rhodes and Theocritus. Odes to Priapus were part of this Alexandrian inheritance. Catullus wrote a lost ode to Priapus. The Satyricon *begins, as a sissy's Iliad, with an invocation to the garden god.*

Among the surviving priapeia, *the most intriguing is this gleefully obscene one by Tibullus, who saw in the little god who stands attention the patron of pedophilia.*

The Poem

What's going on? What are the gods angry about *now*?

A pale boy lay glowing, warm and secret in my lap, around
    us the night blacked out its soundless course.

Love herself rested. My soft old penis went senile, forgetting
    altogether the manly way it used to poke up its head.

Help, Priapus! You, stiffly standing guard under the tree's
    mane of leaves, with your magic red dong at attention,
    the vine-crown on your crimson head.

Didn't I give you simple-hearted worship, circling your hair
    with chains of just-opened flowers?

Well-hung one! Didn't I shout away old Crow and quick
    Jackdaw before they could pickaxe their horny bills into
    your sacred head?

Unspeakable crotch-deserter! This is goodbye. So long,
    Priap, I don't owe you a thing.

I hope you lie rotting in the field, rough and scaly with dirt,
    wild dogs and pigs involved in mud will scratch their
    smeared sides against your wood . . . .

And as for *you* —

Bad penis! Shame on you!

This is terrible. The gods are using you to punish me. Holy
    immortals, your law is good but cruel.

Some complaining's allowed. Poor prick! No skinny-limbed
    little boy will spread for you, a boy who (for all his
    youth) knows just how to tilt his ass and wriggle it
    delightfully back while the bed shakes underneath.

No merry girl will press you in her hands as if to warm you,
    or squeeze you against her smooth white thigh.

But here comes a gal Romulus used to call honey; I see she
    still has both her teeth . . ..
The doorway to her guts hangs open in the black secrecy and
    midnight of her groin,
enlivened by some stray and snowy hairs. A spider web
    spans the long-deserted entrance —
and she's waiting for you! To glom your smooth head down
    the depths of her trench, and not just once.
You don't feel so good? Fine! Lie there, soft as a worm, she
    won't care, she'll just keep stuffing you up, maybe three
    or four times!
Your snootiness will do you lots of good when you're
    dunking your well-traveled head in her slurping muck.
Still sleepy? Had enough of doing nothing?
I'll let you off this once — but when that gold-pale boy
    comes back, when you sense his footsteps, I want
    swelling flesh to shoot you up rigid with joy,
the whole groin's payload aloft, plunging, hard, till
    giggling Venus squirt me soft.

Cerberus

a triple homage to Sextus Propertius

dedicated to
Meryl Gross

I

A Psychic Geography of Masochism

The Masochist as Initiate

Among those who have explored S&M, there is a persistent sense that there is more at stake than intense orgasm and obsessive pleasures. The correspondences with ritual are manifold and persuasive, from the often hieratically stiff choreography of the action to the use of masks. Anthropological parallels between the voluntary suffering of the masochist and that of the initiate are only too well known. Even the fashions favored by the S&M crowd sometimes imitate sincerely (if a bit crudely) the "aboriginal." But the connection has so far been glimpsed only "through a glass darkly."

The map to the S&M labyrinth emerges only if we understand that it resembles in detail a very particular kind of ritual, an initiation — and *initiation is always a symbolic death*. From the Winnebago Indian Medicine Lodge Rite, where the intiate is "shot" with a gun and "dies" before returning to life, to the Turkish dervish sect of the *Bektashi*, who recite from a symbolic gallows, "I die before my death for the love of those who show the truth, in the convent of a saint I become a sacrifice," death is always the content of initiation's symbols. The second-century AD Latin author Apuleius informs us that his initiation into the Isis cult was "like a voluntary death . . . where the initiate treads the very threshold of Proserpine." In his *On the Soul*, the first-century AD Greek encyclopaedist Plutarch notes that the words "to die," *teleutan*, and "to be initiated," *teleisthai*, correspond in sound and meaning. The funereal black clothing of the S&M scene, its fascination with the whip and the rest of the executioner's tools, and of course the central role of pain, all these proclaim that S&M is a symbolic Dance of Death. Numerous ancient statues and proclaim that S&M is a symbolic dance of death. Numerous ancient statues and frescos show Aphrodite holding the sandal she uses to spank Eros, and this sandal is cited in *The Greek Magical Papyri* as a *symbolon*, a token of initiation. The rueful little cupid on the facing page is a punished Eros. The famous whipping scene in the Villa of the Mysteries painting at Pompei puts the S&M content of a Dionysus initiation beyond serious dispute.

The gagged silence of the masochist, the pallor appropriate to the sufferer, his incapacity for movement, the remote location "far from help" where the drama is played out, all these would be recognized by a person from an archaic society as standard initiatory trappings. The initiate, as one symbolically dead, is one removed from society, from the living — though to the jungle depths or a desolate

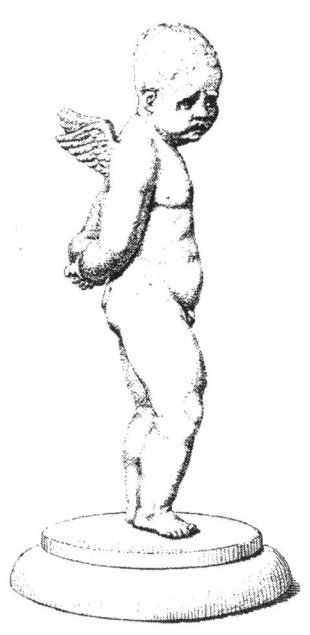

mountaintop instead of a suburban dungeonette. The initiate is made silent and ghostly — though through a vow of silence and whitening of the face rather than by donning a leather hood. The initiate experiences symbolic death agonies — these are commonly circumcision, knocking out of an an incisor, or loss of a digit, though simple flogging is not unusual.

The prime difference is that the literal initiate suffers these things as a means of entering upon transformation and renewal of his entire existential condition, rather than as a way of refreshing a tired sex-life and staving off depression. On the cold crags, in the brutal peace of the wilderness, the primitive and pre-classical Greeks initiated their young men into warrior societies, a custom for which Greek myth gives an attenuated record in the stories of young heros (e.g. Achilles, Jason, Asklepios) being trained in the mountains by centaurs. Similarly the *Yamabushi* ("one who lies in the mountains") of medieval Japan acquired his shamanic powers on mountaintops haunted by ghosts and spirits. The modern myth of the masochist "kidnapped" by the sadist to a remote chateau preserves these otherworld associations with an additional French and Arthurian touch. The purely physical risk is here the least interesting factor. The carrying off of the masochist brings him to *a mode of life that is utterly other, the life of spirits*, and this supplies meaning and power to the scene.

In the dazed resignation of the morning after, the masochist gathers his clothing, too spent to even inspect his new bruises, and little interested in them. Before the inevitable depression sets in — the price of life lived with desacralized intensity — he is drunk with a mood of romantic alienation, self-pity and vague religious longing. The deserted playroom is for him the wild, the shore, the crags, the no-go zone inhabited by wolves and centaurs, what the Roman poet Propertius called "landscapes of abandonment."

The Masochist as Ghost

Much of what is encountered on the journey into S&M sacrifices its opacity as soon as we understand it as a trip into the Land of the Dead. All mythologies describe this as a realm where everything is inverted; as *The Book of Job* expresses it as, "the reversed and backward kingdom where night is day." This is a looking-glass world where the mistress presents the positive to the slave's every negative: her pleasure is his pain, she is clothed and he is naked, she speaks and he is silent. By a slow accumulation of parallels, the slave becomes the reverse and mimic of the mistress.

Once both are moving in perfect sync, when the reflection is flawless, a sharp and sudden pain may bring the slave "through the looking-glass."

In the Egyptian Book of the Dead, a late and elaborate final efflorescence of Nile-side piety, one of the most often iterated charms to stave off the laws of Hell is "I shall not walk upside down, I shall not eat excrement." This underlines in a very striking way the topsy-turvy character of the underworld. Here again, the experience of the masochist is of a piece with that of the dead. The sensations of weightlessness and even of leaping or flying that accompany the endorphin rush are already an adequate translation of "walking upside down." The experience of the "witches' cradle" or flesh-hook suspension makes this point with added clarity.

The labyrinth was well known to the ancients as an emblem of the state where all directions, even up and down, are lost. It was commonly used to represent the underworld journey. To quote again from Plutarch's *On the Soul*, "Initiation and death both begin with weary runnings about in circles, journeys through darkness over uncertain roads and down blind alleys." More modern and more common than the mazes that fascinated the ancients, but equally apt as an emblem of the dead realm, are mirrors. Borges, who wrote with such insight of both mirrors and mazes, speaks in his poem *Los Espejos* of the horror of the reflected world, uninhabitable yet inhabited, repeating our reality with a sleepless and sexual obsessiveness, a place where everything happens and nothing is remembered.

For one who has learned to walk upside down, it is not difficult to understand this "mirror writing." The silent and spaceless depths of the mirrored infinity are at the same time a glimpse of the dead realm and a reflection of the masochist mind, endlessly empty and just as endlessly ready to absorb whatever it is shown.

Yet his corpse-like passivity conceals a richness of interior experience that can scarcely be imagined. Within his silence and immobility he experiences a world whose center is neither pain nor pleasure, but rather the prolonged and overexcited anticipation of both. The classical writers on initiation speak over and over of "joy mixed with dread," "excitement, confusion and hope." An empty, expectant eternity in which all sensations echo, and strong ones overwhelm. Such is the condition of one who has given up all control. And thus the ongoing existential condition of the accomplished masochist (in Propertius' words),

> . . . to live without plans, caution or expectation — to be carried
> at random by whatever happens, without all will or control.

He is a holy wanderer who believes in no god, a quest knight for whom the grail has become irrelevant.

The binding and blindfolding which are standard initiatory procedure are a further assimilation of the slave's condition to that of the dead. He enters the night of non-being, his personality becomes a gap. Slaves often report a sense that their head has vanished or become weightless, that the entire body seems disincorporated, except for the violated genitals and the punished buttocks. "I am nothing but a hole for you to use," the slave may say.

A hole to be used he certainly is, though far from nothing but. As he descends to the world of the dead, as this "journey to the center of the earth" continues, his experience of sex becomes ever more acute, because he is entering the belly of being, the source of all fertility. He sinks, and is all but dissolved into this underearth, sightless and sparkling with the germinal modes of being, the seeds of plantlife and the "growth" of minerals in their now almost pulsing ore-veins. His genitals fiercely tingle, resonant with the terrible fertility of the buried. While the personality and body-sense are lost, the genital region seems to literally seethe with being.

Mastery of Fire

Fire-play, such as the shaman's ability to walk on hot coals, is universally recognized in archaic societies as a spiritual show of force, an indication that one has gone beyond the mortal condition The hot wax play of our time is strikingly paralleled by a number of cultic usages from antiquity, none of which is more strikingly *à propos* than this one taken from the Isis cult. It is enacted as the central scene in novel *The Golden Ass* (written by Apuleius, a priest of Isis). In the central episode of the book, Psyche accidentally *spills hot oil* on Eros in bed. This is paralleled by a number of late antique carved gems, reproduced here, that show Eros and Psyche, interchangeably shackling one another, tying one another to pillars, and scorching one another with fire-brands. A particularly powerful one, reproduced at the beginning of this section, shows Eros holding a butterfly, the symbol of Psyche, over a torch: the illustration that introduces this essay similarly portrays Eros torturing a winged Psyche with fire.

The Hunger of the Dead

"It's difficult to eat shit without having visions," Allen Ginsberg wrote in a burst of poetic intuition. The classically degrading licking of the buttocks, a hardy perennial of all S&M, is a very sufficient actualization of the second half of our Egyptian verse quoted a little earlier, "I shall not eat excrement." The spell was of course meant to prevent the reversal of the normal order in the dead realm, where the mouth may be forced to accept, without demur, dung in place of food. After all, what is buried is not fed but fertilized. We might understand the Egyptian verse in less nightmarish terms as, "I shall not taste my own corruption." The masochist however has wishes most opposite to those of the departed Egyptian: not to maintain life in the world of the dead, but to experience the raptures of annihilation in the world of the living. Thus the masochist's post, on his knees, lapping his mistress' anus, an act whose archetypal power was also appropriated by participants in the witches' Sabbath, and the initiates of the Knights Templar, both of whom made use of the "infernal kiss." The eating of excrement is secretly famous in Indian *Aghori* initiations, as is the ingestion of human flesh from the burning ghats.

66

There the living-dead status of the feaster is well attested, even boasted. But there is more.

"All food comes to us from the world of the dead," declare the Hippocratic writings. The underworld, great granary to every buried seed, is rich in fantasies of being devoured and of monstrous feasting. The dead are at once guarantors of fertilty and monsters of appetite. For this reason the Greeks populated their underworld with never-satisfied ones, ("hungry ghosts" in the Buddhist term), like Tantalus eternally grasping for the unattainable apple. Likewise, the Masochist pays for his overemphasized pleasures with endless yearning, a hunger for sensation and degradation which is finally as insatiable as the grave.

The risk in approaching the world of the unseen is universally acknowledged. Dante suggests he was on the verge of suicide in the opening of the *Commedia*. The walking of the razor-thin *Cinvat* bridge in Iranian myth is the most concise example, but universally the approach to the otherworld is seen as perilous. This ambivalence of the sacred is to be understood as the implicit dread that the approach to the holy will rob one of the ability to return to the mundane, the everyday, if you will, the "vanilla" world. In the event, a very well-founded fear, if one is not too literal in one's understanding.

S&M has similar connotations of danger, and attempts by the kinky community to allay popular disquiet, to be seen as having made a "normal lifestyle choice," are on one level misguided. Fear is the ambiance, even the lifeblood of S&M. It is this which makes the journey a quest, and not merely tourism. And the unacknowledged secret of the masochist's gloomy pride is death. Few there are who will ever pursue the implications of masochism even so far as castration, but the ultimate extension of the masochistic dream is to die, to be devoured, to be incorporated. To have the expiring contractions of the genitals coax an orgasm from the mistress and in a dying convulsion to become fully one with her pleasure: this is the subterranean and electric current that makes masochist limbs twitch with ecstasy. As the Catechism of the Roman Church puts it: "Love seeks to be definitive and irrevocable."

II
The Case of Propertius.

Propertius, an early first-century AD Roman erotic poet, was in many ways the heir of Catullus. He emulated Catullus' highly personal, even neurotic, voice, and the masochism that was an element in Catullus' relationship with Lesbia provided the pattern for Propertius' affair with Cynthia.

Propertius, bard of the bent, has been censored even more dilligently than Catullus: the poet-classicist A. E. Houseman actually rewrote the problematic parts of Propertius, and his bowdlerized edition has pretty much replaced the original for classicists. Decent Shropshire lad!

The content of Propertius' work was not a point wasted on Rome's foremost specialist on sexual play, the poet Ovid: he characterized Propertius poems as "white hot." Nor did Propertius himself show any shyness about his masochism: he calls his love-life an "untreatable medical condition."

The characteristic features of masochism provide the contours of Propertius' world. There is the exceptional importance of fantasy in a sexual scenario; the focus on neither pain nor pleasure as such, but on a prolonged *anticipation* of both; an exhibitionistic desire to be shamed and exposed, a manipulative provocation of others to provide the desired ill-treatment; the subversive use the of punishment as a secret path to pleasure. This checklist may be verified by even a meagre and random sampling of Propertius' poems.

But Propertius is far more than a case history. His poetic genius made his sexual perversion a path to the transcendent; he appropriated the symbols of initiation which, as a classical pagan, he found ready to hand.

The initiate's isolation can be glimpsed even in the way Propertius exulted in the fact his love was, to ordinary persons, incomprehensible: his pride in his otherness. He represented this separateness with a special kind of nature image — scenes of splendid desolation and aloof sublimity which remind one forcibly of those favored by the alienated lovers of the nineteenth century: think of the alpine peaks and ruined cathedrals of Caspar David Friedrich.

Propertius keeps finding himself in *deserta loca*, "landscapes of abandonment." These settings fascinated Propertius' hero Catullus: Attis castrated and alone on the shore of Asia Minor, or Ariadne "on the beachhead of nowhere." I need hardly remind the reader that Attis and Ariadne are the heroes of initiation myths and mystery religions, the cults of Cybele and Dionysus respectively. The Gethsamene-like solitude of the scenes Propertius favored is part of a religious *passion*.

Propertius' frank enjoyment of pain also has overtones of sacrality. His sufferings are tokens of the self's annihilation. The honorable wounds of bedtime scuffles, along with the daily abasements, belittlings and humiliations of his relationship with Cynthia, amounted to a kind of initiatory ordeal — they had an existential meaning: they alone made him feel real. As he candidly declares, he will accept any diminution of his own status, become no more than Cynthia's *imago*, her shadow, her echo, her ghost, because doing so gives him *a kind of immortality*. Her love brings him across the river Styx,

> "There in the world of the dead, whatever I still am, I will always be called a ghost that belongs to you."

In one poem Propertius says he would gladly be dead if only she'd pity him, or better still, actively abuse him. Let her at least dance beside his pyre and trample his bones! — an image which calls to mind the dancing Kali of the burning ghats.

Elsewhere Propertius says, "Venus seized me, roasted me in her cruel cauldron." The equation of passionate and physical fire — already implicit in the Latin word *ardor* — is absolute.

Propertius was a helpless devotee of the archetype of the powerful woman, the kind who could, as he says, "use her will to leash in untamed men." The theme of bad, powerful women recurs obsessively — Cleopatra, Scylla, Tarpeia — the names are a rosary of overheated submissive cravings. These far outshine the fulsome hymns he was required to write to his patron and emperor. Augustus was a tyrant, but unlike Cynthia, a very uninspiring one. One of the most poignant lines in Propertius' last book is this tribute to the defeated Cleopatra,

> . . . her shattered scepter swept along on the waves of
> Ionia's sea . . .

Propertius, focusing on this trivial and melancholy detail evokes a mood of dreamy regret at the loss to the world of this imperious woman, and so effectively overshadows the whole poem that is its context, an officially commissioned glory-song on Augustus and the battle of Actium.

Thus the symbolism of the mistress ceaselessly re-surfaces in Propertius' verse. In one poem he says, "Cynthia was the first, and she shall be the last." This may be taken literally — *au pied de la lettre* — she is for him the Alpha and Omega of a personal religion of sex.

But Propertius desired more than mere eternity: the masochistic fantasy of enslavement, of being owned, reached in him a febrile apotheosis in dreams of total incorporation and personal extinction Thus he imagined the ghost of Cynthia saying,

> Other women may have you now, but soon you're mine alone.
> Sexual craving, an immortal force, shall make our bodies jog
> > together even after death
> in an awful and inanimate copulation
> till the dry grind of bone on bone at last confounds us into one
> > common heap of dust.

III
Selected Poems of Propertius

Mental Illness

Cynthia was the first – she made me her moping prisoner
    with a single indifferent glance.
I'd never before been infected by love or gotten sick with
    desire —
Love slapped my smirk and taught my confident eyes to
    stare submissively groundwards,
Love, like a wrestler, threw me down, set his foot on my
    head to show he'd beaten me completely,
nasty Love trained me to despise nice girls
and to live without plans, caution or expectation — to be
    carried at random by whatever happens, without all will
    or control.
This isn't "a phase" — it's mental illness — it's gone on a
    whole year without easing up
even though it angers all the gods — at me — and ruins my
    life, I'm forced, I have no choice.

Still, Milanion won the fierce man-hating heart of the
    huntress Atalanta
because he never backed away from any labor or pain: love-
    crazed, he would wander looking for her, checking every
    cave in her native Arcadia in case she was hiding out
    there.
Instead of her , he met huge, shaggy, fanged wild
    animals,
fought two centaurs who were trying to rape her, and
    though he won, he got such a crack from the one
    centaur's club
he lay for days groaning on the bare Arcadian rock.

It took the sight of his agony to overtake the affections of the
    girl who outran all her would-be   lovers:
just begging her, working for her, deserving her –
that didn't get him far.

With me, Love becomes stupid, he doesn't think up plans,
can't even remember what worked in the past.

Witches, you who claim to pull the moon down to earth,
who fuss over ugly offerings made on altars of underworld
    gods —
see if your power's great enough to turn *my* Cynthia's
    thoughts to me,
make her go pale as I am now, all sick from loving her.
Do that and I'll believe you when you say your chantings
    can whirl the stars backwards down the night sky, that
    you can send rivers gushing in reverse all the way back
    to their source!

My friends, who call down (too late!) to me who've fallen so
    far
and lie here now so weak — find me, my friends, a medicine
    to heal my mind diseased —
I'm brave enough for the scalpel, sear out the sick with red-
    hot iron —
if only I could once more feel and speak my anger like a free
    man —
I've been her slave so long I can't remember how —
then take me to earth's furthest verge, beyond all inhabited
    regions,
take me somewhere no woman can ever track me down —

But it's safe for you to keep living here, you shallow happy
people,
who've found your little likeness of a lovemate, your sweet
peer and equal, who the gods brought you just 'cause
you asked — live sappily ever after!
The Venus who rules over my kind keeps my nights busy
with misery,
every hour empty and full of longing.

Keep back — it could be infectious, stay where you are,
mind your own business, stick to your steady reliable
kind of love —
don't read any further — but, if caution bores you and
you're already skimming obliviously ahead,
I promise this warning will come back to you in total recall,
bitterly vivid, loud and clear as pain.

Ariadne

Like exhausted Ariadne as she lay asleep on Crete's deserted
    shores while the ship of Theseus — who swore he'd be
    her lover — withdrew further off and ever smaller on the
    sea;
or like Andromeda, daughter of Ethiopian king Cephys,
    rescued by Perseus,
like Andromeda laid out by the onset of the first sleep she'd
    known since she was chained to the rough rocks, waiting
    to be eaten by the dragon of the sea;
or like a Thracian bacchante, who's danced in assiduous
    ecstasy all the way down into Thessaly,
when she collapses on the grassy banks of the Apidanus;
that's how Cynthia seemed, breathing soft and even, head
    laid on her folded hands,
when I dragged my drunken footsteps home, much of
    Bacchus still in me,
the night near gone, my slaves waving spent torches to keep
    them lit.

I tried to draw close to her, carefully sustaining my weight
    on the bed so as not to press on her
— I hadn't got entirely witless with drink. But even though
    doubly inflamed and driven
by Love and Bacchus, both hard demanding gods,
to gently slip my arm beneath her and tilt her head towards
    me, to steal a few belated kisses,
still, I didn't dare disturb my mistress' rest, afraid of her
    scolding, the cruelty I've learned to expect;
so I just stood there, unable to turn away, staring,
    hypnotized, like Argus — all eyes —

like Argus when Juno set him guard over Inachus' daughter
    Io,
Jove's girlfriend-turned-heifer now marveling at the odd feel
    of having horns.

I was taking the garland from my forehead
and putting it, Cynthia, over your temples;
I delighted in curling 'round my fingers your locks that had
    slipped down;
now I was setting apples in the hollow of your palms,
but all these gifts I lavished on your ungrateful slumber
kept rolling down the slopes of your clothing,
and whenever you moved a little or caught your breath
I was startled — like a fool when he hears his fortune told —
afraid some creature of dream brought you surreal terrors,
afraid someone in your sleep made you, unwilling, his.

Meanwhile, the descending moon shone in through
    successive windows,
advancing in haste, yet slow to withdraw its radiant gaze,
    reluctant to miss a bit of this,
finally its gentle rays shone full on your closed eyes, woke
    you.
One elbow propped on the pillow, you sat up and said,

"So you finally decided to give *my* bed a try? You must have
    gotten thrown out of whoever else's house, and that only
    after insults failed to give you the hint!
Where was it you used up the whole night that should have
    been mine, coming back exhausted when the stars are
    already vanishing?
Scumbag! *You* should spend evenings like mine, and know
    what kind of misery you're always putting me through.

I tried to cheat sleep out of the hours till you came, now at
    the loom, now blearily reading poems composed on
    Orpheus' lyre,
now whispering to myself how you'd abandoned me, how
I'm always left waiting while you romance someone new;
finally sleep pushed me down with his sweet soft wing — I
    was crying, crying,
crying over you."

Battle

I loved trading punches with you last night at the hour when
    lamps are lit,
sweet on my ears were your screams and curses, dear to me
    your insanity
when, raging with wine, you overturned the table and
    pitched full glasses at me with adorable mad hands.
I really want you to yank my hair — attack it!
Score my face with your beautiful nails,
tell me how you'll put out torches in my eye-sockets,
tear my clothes, make me stand bare for you to punish.
These and these alone are sure signs of true love;
no woman's feelings be so deeply hurt unless she cared.
The woman whose lips are spitting insults at you
grovels and writhes with passion at great Venus' feet.

Whether she's walking stately with full entourage, or
    whether she plunges off by herself
running through the streets like a crazed bacchante;
whether she's unbalanced and trembling (as often) from
    nightmares, or from jealousy —
sometimes just a *picture* of another girl's enough.
I'm the astrologer to read the night sky that is her mind.
I've learned these details form the constellation that is Love.
If she doesn't care enough to have screaming fights, she
    doesn't care about you much at all.
A woman who's even-tempered, calm — that is, dull — is
    what I wish for my enemies.
I want my friends to see teethmarks on my neck, I want
    bruises for proof she's been with me, is   mine,
what I want out of love is pain, and if I can't have that,

at least I want to learn that *she's* in pain.

If I can't have my tears, then I want yours.
When you look at me in that certain kind of way, glaring
    from under your eyebrows,
when your fingers tell me in sign-language something really
    unprintable,
then I pity those whose dreams aren't punctuated by gasps.
I always want to be pale with fear before an angry woman.

Paris enjoyed the sweetest of passions — how I envy the
    man —
able to take his pleasure with Helen in earshot of armor's
    crash!
While the Greeks advanced and Hector stood firm, he
    soldiered nobly on between Helen's legs—
like Paris, I make love while I make war.

I'm always off to battle — with you or with my rivals.
I don't *want* a truce.
So be glad there's no woman as beautiful as you — you'd
    surely grieve if there were —
be arrogant! you're entitled!
But as for *you*, who try to snare my girl, I wish you eternal
    in-laws!
And if she lets you steal a night with her, it isn't that she
    likes you, she's only mad at me.

Ghosts

So ghosts really do exist! Death isn't the end of it all, it
    seems some pallid shadow escapes, defeating the pyre –
for I just saw Cynthia, buried in a quiet spot far from the
    noisy highway,
I saw Cynthia leaning over me.
I'd only now returned from the funeral and sadly had the
    whole cold bed to myself
(unhappy king of a frigid new domain),
an uneasy sleep of erotic dreams descended on me
    tentatively.

Her hair was the same as when they carried her away,
her eyes too, but the fire'd scorched her dress on one side.
The heat had dulled and cracked the beryl she always wore
    on her finger.
Her lips had shriveled back a little from the touch of Lethe
    water,
but awareness still breathed through her and sent forth a
    voice
— though the fingers of her flame-desiccated hand made a
    grating sound.

"You bastard! not much hope you'll be nicer to another girl
    —
look at you, fast asleep and me just this minute buried!
Have you already forgotten our stolen gaudy nights in the
    after-hours taverns?
My windowsill worn smooth from all the times I lowered
    myself by a rope, hand over hand, into your arms?

How many times did we worship Venus at the crossroads,
	body hot against body, paving-stones warming under
	your back?
But the loyalty was somewhat less than a tacit
	understanding — or maybe the south wind, that neither
	hears nor cares, just blew your lies away!

No one screamed my name when my eyes began to close —
If you'd called out to me, I might have wheedled at least one
	further day of life —
and no one hired a watcher to sit by my corpse all night with
	a rattle to scare off soul-stealing	demons.
That cheap undertaker propped my head up with a piece
	of broken roof-tile that made a gash in my scalp.
But the worst is: no one saw *you* doubled over with grief, or
	soaking your toga with hot real tears.

If it was too much trouble to follow the mourners beyond
	the gate, you could at least have ordered them to slow
	down a bit!
Couldn't you have even expressed the conventional wish
	that the winds should fan my pyre
to release my soul quickly from its corpse?
Ingrate! and why didn't you sprinkle some incense on my
	bier to sweeten the flames?
Would it have strained your finances to pluck a few wild
	hyacinths and toss them on?
To shatter a jar of common wine at the graveside to honor
	my demise?

I want to sear that slave Lygdamus, heat a knife and torture
	out the truth—

when he gave me that cup of greenish wine I should have
  known it was a trap!
Or maybe it was the housekeeper, Nomas? Say she already
  ditched the secret fatal flavoring she slipped in my food,
a heated shard of crockery sizzling into her skin will make
  her damn her own guilty hands!
She used to be displayed in front of a brothel, and not that
  long ago, for nights of pleasure, cheap.
But now she'll scarcely honor the humble ground with the
  trailing golden hem of her gown!

Yet for all that, she still makes sure, as she hands out unfair
  wool-baskets for the evening's spinning,
that an extra-heavy one goes to any maid so loose-tongued
  as to comment on how pretty I was.
And she made sure old Petala felt her wrists roped tight to
  the filthy whipping post
for hanging wreaths on my gravestone, and Lalaga
was tied upright, her long braids bound to an overhanging
  beam,
and beaten — because she asked a favor with the phrase
  Cynthia always used to let me. . .
And this same Nomas, as soon as I was dead, you allowed to
  take that gold portrait bust of me
and use it for her dowry, why you practically melted it
  down for money in the flames of my pyre!

But, much as you deserve it, Propertius, I'm not going to
  keep harassing you.
Long was my rule in the realm of your poems.
I swear by the song the Fates chant, which brings events into
  irrevocable being

— so may the three-headed hell-hound bark softly in my
    hearing —
I was always true to you. If I lie may vipers slip
hissing through my tomb and nap curled around my bones!

The proof is: there are two abodes assigned along that nasty
    river;
large as the crowd of shadows is, they've only two possible
    directions to row.
This way the wave leads to the husband-killing adulteress
Clytemnestra, and the Cretan queen Pasiphae, who hid
    naked
in a hollow wooden cow to see what it was like to get
    crammed by a bull;
but to where I am, the other half flies in a yacht festooned
    with flowers,
here holy breezes stroke the roses of Elysium
in a harmony of harps, to the round bronze cymbals
of Cybele, among the turbaned Lydian mystics
plucking lyres as they dance: these are the initiates.
There's Andromeda, who almost ended up fish-bait;
Hypermestra, who alone out of fifty sisters,
didn't gut her husband on the group-wedding night
(she actually did love the man she'd just married).
These heroic blameless wives don't mind retelling the
    famous moments of their lives.
Andromeda describes how, served up for the sea monster,
    her wrists were bruised by chains her own mother'd
    locked on,
it felt cold, that wet rock, beneath her innocent fingers.
Hypermestra modestly asserts it was only lack of courage
that kept her from daring to go along with her sisters in their
    supposedly noble deed.

Thus we continue, though dead, to hallow with our tears the
   loves we knew in life.
And me, I keep quiet — about all your vicious betrayals!

Now I'm giving you some instructions, that is, if you still
   feel anything for me,
if that bitch Choris' love-potions don't control you utterly:
see to it my nurse Parthenia, shaky with age, doesn't want
   for anything
(she never made you bribe her to get in to see me, though
   she surely had the chance),
and my dear maid Felicity — my "perfect felicity" — free
   her. I don't want her handing
another mistress the mirror. And any of your poems
that gained an easy dactyl from my name – burn them, a
   sacrifice to me!
Why should you get a free ride from my reputation?
And pull that ivy off my tomb! I don't want its twisty
   tendrils eating into my tender skeleton as it swells its
   berries. Ah, my sweet grave,
where the orchard-bordered river Anio stretches sleepily out
   among the fields
in a landscape sacred to Hercules, through whose magic
   power the air's so pure that ivory never   discolors
there.
I want you to honor me by setting up a column, inscribing
   'round its middle these brief but well-earned verses –
and carve them large enough so a messenger running from
   Rome can read them as he gallops past:

Here, in the soil of Tivoli, lies magnificent Cynthia,
adding, River Anio, new glory to your banks.

Don't dismiss this dream that comes through the gate of
  holy visions!
Such dreams are truthful, sacred and weighty!
By night we ghosts are wafted off to wander, night frees the
  shut-in shades, and once the bolt shoots back
even Cerberus roves. But the eternal law of daylight
  commands us return to Lethe lagoon.
A careful Charon counts the whole boatload, back we go.
Other women may have you now, but soon you're mine
  alone.
Sexual craving, an immortal force, shall make our bodies jog
  together even after death
in an awful and inanimate copulation
till the dry grind of bone on bone at last confounds us into
  one common heap of dust."

When she'd run through every complaint in this indictment,
she vanished and my arms hugged nothingness.

The Rout

Listen and learn of last night's rout, what sent folk running
  past the aqueducts and though the new park all the way
  down Esquiline hill!

About twenty miles southeast from Rome on the Appian
  Way is the town Lanuvium,
with an ancient shrine to Juno the Defender, watched over
  since forever by a giant snake.
It's well worth stopping by once a year to see the rite.
  There's a black chasm in the sacred hillside, jagged as if
  it had been torn open,
and into it goes an offering made in honor of the hungry
  serpent,
down such a path as even pure guiltless virgins should
  hesitate to travel.
The monster twists and hisses from the depths of the earth to
  ask for its yearly provisions
and the young girls sent in to perform this rite go terror-
  white,
the baskets shake in their arms
as they trust unprotected fingers to that scaly mouth.
He snaps up the morsels they hold out to him. If the
  maidens are chaste,
they return to their parents' hugs and the farmers shout, *A
  year of good crops!*

Cynthia rode off to see this, in a carriage drawn by newly-
  groomed ponies,
to honor Juno — she said — but Venus is more whom she
  had in mind.

Tell me, I implore, O Appian Way, for you were witness to
    her triumphal progress,
how she drove, wheels a blur of rattling speed, down your
    paving stones;
disclose the squalid brawls she caused in the small-town
    taverns en route,
(I didn't even have to be along for her to humiliate me!).
What a noble sight she must have been, leaning forward like
    a racing charioteer and flicking the reins to speed her
    horses on to the next rough bar!
I'm not even going to mention her girl-faced friend, that
    high-living young heir who rides in a carriage with a silk
    awning
like a wealthy woman who fears the sun might give her
    freckles.
Did he bring along his Molossian lapdogs — who wear
    bracelets for collars?
— he'll have to sell himself into slavery for a piece of moldy
    bread
by the time that manhood he's so ashamed of can't be
    hidden no matter how close the razor scrapes.

In view of all these outrages to my bed and my affections,
I thought I'd pack my gear and try fighting on another front.
There's a certain Phyllis who lives near Diana's temple on
    Aventine hill,
no delight when she's sober, but if she drinks, she shines,
    whatever the setting.
The other is Teia from Tarpeian grove — a cheerful
    unaffected girl
— and once she's drunk — one man's not enough.
I decided to invite them and charm away the night
    refreshing my love-life with a few new adventures.

There was a single banqueting couch for the three of us in
    my secluded garden.
As for the seating arrangement: I lay between the two of
    them.
Lygdamus wielded the ladle, filling the summer glassware
    with the Grecian refinement of a fine Lesbian wine.
The flutist came from the Nile's banks; Phyllis danced with
    castanets
and so neatly, with so natural a grace, we couldn't help
    showering her with roses.
But though the lamps were full, the light kept flickering. The
    table fell over, back flat and legs in the air.
And me, try as I might to roll the seven sacred to Venus with
    my lucky dice — the ominous snake-eyes kept glaring up
    at me.
The girls sang for a deaf man, showed their breasts to one
    blind.
In my mind I was alone, waiting at the gates of Lanuvium.

Suddenly *our* outer gates screeched on rust-hoarse hinges,
we heard a faint bustle — something flying up the path —
and there on the threshold was Cynthia! The dining-room
    doors slammed flat to the wall on either side of her
like dreadful big wings. Her hair wasn't in its usual careful
    array,
but beautifully insane — it really looked great.
My fingers went weak and let the cup drop; my lips,
though steeped in wine enough to slur my words, went
    white with terror.
Her eyes flashed out dire sparkles, she was raging in that
    infinite way only women can.

91

The sight of a besieged city's fall could not have been more
	awesome.
Cynthia leapt, talons out, for Phyllis' face — a terrified Teia,
	to get the neighbors, screamed *Fire!*
Lamps appeared in the dark street's loud confusion,
	yawning bleary citizens doddered out of their houses
as my girls, with hair pulled and clothes torn, ran down the
	road to the first open tavern and dove in.
Cynthia exulted in her spoils — the rags ripped from their
	dresses — and gashed my face with a sidelong swipe of
	her hand.
She sunk a set of bleeding teethprints in my neck
and especially tried for my eyes "that like to look at other
	women."

Then, when she'd smacked me till her arms were tired,
she dragged out Lygdamus (he'd hid under the banqueting
	couch).
The prostrating slave grabbed my knees and in that pose of
	worship
begged me to save him, as though I were a god.
What could I do, Lygdamus? I was just as much her prisoner
	of war as you.

Hands up, I made unconditional surrender.
She pointed to her feet, then barely let me kiss them, and
	said,
"If you wish me to pardon your confessed offense,
accept my judgment and obey it's stipulations!

You're not to put on your best clothes and stroll in the shade
	of Pompey's colonnade,

nor in the forum when they spread sand in the streets to
  make them look neat for a holiday.
You're never again to swivel your head for sneaky backward
  glances
in the theatre, to see what pretty girls are in the back row,
or on the street, when the curtain parts on a woman's
  covered litter
— no loitering! And above all Lygdamus, your slave and
  your corrupter,
is to have his ankles manacled and be sold on the auction
  block."
She laid down the law. I accepted. She laughed, proud of the
  power I gave up to her.
Then she sprayed perfume on any place the strange girls
  might have touched, scrubbed the threshold with
  springwater,
and ordered the oil and wicks in all the lamps to be changed;
she fumigated my head three times with smoldering sulfur
and changed every sheet on the bed. After all this solemn
  exorcism,
I said "amen" — and we made peace — all over the bed.

The Rotting Goddess

Dedication
To Hecate

Pre-Christian, pre-Olympian, pre-Titanic Hecate
world-tree planted in Asia Minor,
gate-guard of the worlds,
keyholder to the three realms,
gross seated Mother, lions at your sides,
fostering nurse of all that's young,
female heap of big fat attributes,
cruel, non-rational mistress
of slain corn-kings, sacrificed children,
castrated temple-males;

you glid into Greece after Troy's fall,
Hecate-Enodia riding down from Thessaly,
leading the angry horde of ghosts,
planted yourself at the crossroads;
your torch began to smoke, then flared up,
making night noon —
world-tree Hecate, your roots reached Hell's
downmost altitude to suck the power
of the buried dead. Eater of filth,
goddess of darkness, grimly silently
munching corpses, Hecate,
regaled with incense of goat-fat, baboon-shit,
garlic; honored with gutted puppies
and rubbish rites;

Hecate, in your oak-leaf crown shaking reptile dreadlocks,
around you hell-hounds yowling sharp and shrill,

so meadows tremble, river-nymphs scream,
their waters rush backwards up the stream-bed
and dive affrighted down their own fountains;

with the witches I dance around you,
naked, snake-necklaced,
hair in the wind, gashing blood from arms:
sex-crazed hags with false teeth and hair,
young girls, gloriously pornographic,
stir the cauldron of ugly oddities,
throw in magic salads gathered in the graveyard
— a brew with power to draw babes screaming
into existence, or hurl them howling hence.
The witches lay hold of you, Hecate, World-tree,
shake, make tremble on your branches
the planets suspended
like rare and fragile fruit.

Introduction

Strange to say, witchcraft in antiquity is a subject which has never been seriously studied. The books on witchcraft all begin with the middle ages, and blandly assume that the witches of Rome were not materially different from their sisters in Salem. Studies of magic in antiquity, of which there are more than a few, do not recognize witchcraft for a practice with precisely defined means and goals.

Now, while it is true that every witch uses magic, not every magician is a witch. As long as the definition and limits of witchcraft remain unfathomed, analysis remains superficial and is generally made tributary to discussion of such ill-posed and insoluble questions as "the difference between magic and religion."

The textual commentaries and studies of specific classical authors who depict witches confine themselves, without exception, to literary analysis, offering no more than citations of this or that motif in other writers, without meaningful examination.

Hecate has similarly been slighted as a subject, and for the same general reasons. The medievalists who write on witchcraft or its goddess are, as a rule, neither interested nor versed in the ancient world, while classicists typically have little taste for anything smacking of Christendom. Thus the triple goddess finds herself in a scholarly no-man's-land.

And there she remains, despite the discoveries in this volume, which appeared in scholarly journals and then in book form more than a decade ago. This is due in part to the conservatism of classical philologists, but far more to fifty years of ever diminishing of funding for higher education, particularly the humanities, in America. More predictable research on duller subjects than mine has failed to garner recognition or reward in this era of information, our present very well-lit Dark Ages.

Here you will find (still) for the first time a complete and comprehensive study of Hecate and the witches for the 1200 year period from Homer to *The Greek Magical Papyri* (800 BC-400 AD), citing all substantial classical references and offering cross-cultural parallels to support my inferences.

I shall show the slow stages by which Hecate was demonized and the mythology of the evil witch arose, and how, hundreds of years later, the actual practice of witchcraft developed, realizing the troubled dreams of the poets. I shall stand at the moonlit crossroads of the mind and make the so far reluctant spirits chirp to us the secrets of their source and mysteries of their being.

Part One:
Hecate

She is a Tree of Life

"She is a tree of life . . . " — Proverbs 3:18

Hecate's powers date "from the very beginning," Hesiod informs us, in his seventh-century BC poem *The Theogony*, and we may perhaps take him literally. Even though the detailed features of Hecate are lost in the "dark backward and abysm of time," much may be responsibly inferred from her geography, which alone suggests pre-Olympian, Pre-Titanic and even primaeval origin.

An impressive quantity of coins, statues, reliefs and dedications, along with the literary record, place Hecate's origin in Carian Asia Minor (southeastern Turkey), with an important sanctuary at Lagina. In Caria, Hecate enjoyed considerable dignity and political importance — she was protectress of the city of Stratonicea, together with Zeus, and was prominently worshiped alongside various other deities including Gaia. Hecate's veneration elsewhere in the vicinity included initiatory cults on Aegina and Samothrace.

Through classical times her influence spread only westward, affecting some Aegean islands *en route*. Though there is almost no trace of her cult in the Peloponessus (southern Greece), she was immensely popular in Athens and Boeotia. Thus it comes about that she is the subject of the lovely, if somewhat colorless, hymn in Hesiod's *Theogony*, and has a small part in the contemporary Homeric *Hymn to Demeter*. A temple to Hecate stood outside the Eleusis sanctuary at the end of the Sacred Road.

Asia Minor (Turkey), Hecate's oldest known address, hosted the most impressively developed of the Near Eastern neolithic cultures, one with archaeologically and iconographically demonstrable links to the paleolithic. This is attested by the famous discovery of a neolithic metropolis at Çatal Hüyük in Turkey — only 200 miles from Hecate's great temple at Lagina. It is tempting to imagine that Hecate could be traced back to such a giddy antiquity as Çatal Hüyük records, all the way to 3000 BC!

The Indo-European Hittites moved into Asia Minor in the third millenium, just as the neolithic was ending, and the Phrygians in turn established their kingdom there by about 800 BC. This succession of conquests makes it unlikely that Hecate is a goddess who comes down to us unchanged from the furthest past. But even if we assume Hecate was a late Phrygian import, she may plausibly be supposed to have inherited some very ancient traits of the fertility goddesses who figure so prominently in every period of Asia Minor's archaeology, of whom Cybele and Artemis of Ephesus are well known examples.

How may we bring detail to these vague associations? No clarity emerges from Hecate's marginal role in mystery religion — tantalizing as it is, the evidence we have of Hecate in the Eleusis cult and of her role in the Magic and Orphism in late antiquity is too scanty to help. Hecate's name has defied etymology. But the record of Hecate's depiction rises from the ocean of the unknowable like an island on the horizon.

The earliest Hecate image of all is a small sixth-century BC terra-cotta figure of an enthroned goddess, that we can identify as Hecate only because her name is inscribed on it. There are some other early images of Hecates on vases — a generic, Artemis-like figure, securely identifiable only where her name accompanies her image.

Around 430 BC the cult of Hecate was officially established at Athens, and the great sculptor Alcamenes, student of Phidias, created an image of Hecate that would become iconic. He represented her, for the first time, *in triple form*. Though Alcamenes' sculpture did not survive, there are literally hundreds of later copies and imitations of it.

Hecate as she appears in the Hymn to Demeter, holding torches and helping Hermes lead Persephone up out of Hades while Demeter, far right, looks on. A red-figure vase from the fifth century AD.

The Hecate images based on Alcamenes' creation show three identical goddesses ranged around a pillar, either staring out, standing archaically stiff amid the flutings of their robe-folds, or striding in a circle like disquieted caryatids. The only distinguishing marks among the triads are the articles they hold — torch, libation bowl, fruit — and the dogs at their feet. Not until the Roman period do the figures become distinct in figure and dress. For the moment we need only concern ourselves with the unprecedented tripling.

Classical Hecate: a Roman copy, reproducing a Hecate which is probably fairly close to the way Alcamenes represented her.

The clue is the central column, an ever present element, rather thinner in the earliest examples but gradually taking on girth until, by Roman times, it has more the appearance of a pillar than a pole.

The earliest *hekataion* (image of Hecate) was a probably a post or pole hung with three wooden masks, set up at the crossroads Why not four masks, it may be asked. Well, the common terms for the crossroads, in Greek (*triodos*) as in Latin (*trivium*), literally mean "intersection of *three* roads." The idea here is very archaic, and not strictly numerical. The common Indo-European culture from which both the Greek and the Latin descend, viewed the number three as symbolic of "many" or "all." It was the most magical and all-inclusive number. The crossroads and Hecate were visualized as triple to indicate the ability to lead *everywhere*.

The first century AD Roman poet Ovid writes:

> Look at Hecate, standing guard at the crossroads, one face looking in each direction.

The first-century BC Roman encyclopedist Varro confirms that a Hecate image was a common feature of intersections in Greek towns. Plutarch, the first-century BC Greek historian, tells us that the purpose of these images was to provide magic protection to travelers.

A scholiast (ancient commentator) on Aristophanes' play *Lysistrata* supplies the further fact that a *hekataion* is an image of Hecate *carved out of wood*.

Three views of another Roman copy. Cruder in execution, the greater prominence of the pillar is worth noting. The *herm* (representation of Hermes as a sacred fertility pole) alongside Hecate, visible on the right of the far left figure and the left of the far-right figure, is worth noting.

Putting together all our clues, (pole, placement at intersection, facing in all directions, made of wood) a post hung with masks seems a secure conjecture for the archaic *hekataion's* form.

Finally, as Phidias is famous for giving idealised human form to the gods, it is plausible that his student Alcamenes would similarly have transformed Hecate from a mask-rack to full and triple figures.

At this point we are equipped to proceed from the exoteric, historical and archaeological details of Hecate to the genuine mysteries of her being.

Roman copy of a Hecate from about the second century BC, judging by the greater movement shown in the figures. Even though they are already dancing around a column, column-tops are set on the heads to identify them with the column itself.

Artemis is the first goddess with whom Hecate was associated, and the one with whom she came to be most frequently and characteristically syncretized. Artemis herself was, like her brother Apollo, originally from Asia Minor, where she was a fertility goddess. This is visibly clear from her famous Ephesian cult image — the goddess with the many breasts.

At some point before the Greek literary record began, Artemis and Apollo were naturalized as Greek deities, and rapidly cleaned up to suit Greek religious tastes. Artemis was relieved of her inconvenient and perpetual maternity to become a virgin huntress, a fit sister for the young god Apollo.

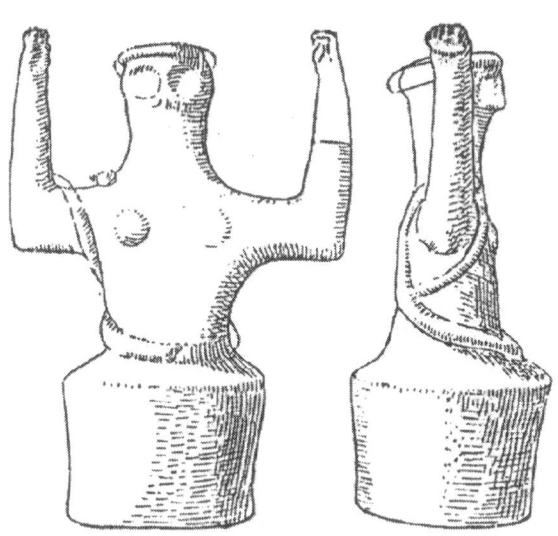

"Tubular idol" from Crete, front and side view, probably from about 1600 BC.

Hecate was also originally a great mother (as I shall demonstrate below), and was similarly being adapted to Greek religion. A certain amount of confusion arose between Hecate and Artemis before their Greek identities were fully defined Thus in fifth century BC, the Greek playwright Aeschylus has the chorus in *The Suppliants* pray that *Artemis-Hecate* may grant the women easy childbirth!

That Hecate was originally a Great Mother in Asia Minor is abundantly attested by epithets, inscriptions and images there; the Greeks frequently compared her to Cybele the *Magna Mater*, and Hesiod, in *The Theogony*, says of Hecate:

> . . . as for those whose business is in waves of the grey and dangerous sea,
> who pray to Hecate and the loud-crashing Earth-Shaker Poseidon,
> easily the glorious goddess Hecate gives them a great catch,
> and easily she takes it away as soon as they see it, if she so wills.
> Along with Hermes, she blesses the barns and makes the cattle increase,
> and wide herds of goats and flocks of fleecy sheep too, if she wills,
> she increases from a few, or makes many less.
> So then, albeit her mother's only child, without brothers to enforce her rights,
> she is honored amongst all the deathless gods. And the son of Kronus, Zeus, has made her, since she was born,
> a fostering nurse to all young creatures whose eyes see the light of all-seeing Dawn.
> So, from the very beginning, she is a nurse of the young, and these are her honors.

Strong testimony, this. But even stronger attestation of Hecate's role as fertility goddess comes from the central pole of the *hekataion*.

Cretan seals from about the sixteenth century BC. Left, the "Mother of the Mountains." The same idea appears to the right in a design that replaces the lion-flanked goddess with a lion-flanked pillar.

To understand this we may look at the parallel provided by the *Asherah* or sacred pole fetish of the Hebrew fertility goddess Ashtoreth, which the Bible informs us was "made of wood" and "cut into shape by man;" scholars believe it must have been a kind of post or stake.

We possess ceramic equivalents of the *Asherah* pole in the many hundreds of terra-cotta figures excavated in Israel alone (similar idols are found throughout the Nile-to-Oxus region) that show a female form with protruding breasts, who is from the waist down a straight cylindrical column with a flared base.

The pillar form of the Egyptian goddess of fertility Hathor is familiar to all visitors of the great museums. Crete had a version as well in the "tubular idols," while many Mycenean gems show, between two lions, interchangeably, a goddess or a pillar.

The pillar at the center of the *hekataion* is not then just a decorative or compositional feature, but may plausibly be taken as an emblem of the goddess herself — the masks or maidens around it are personified extensions of the underlying reality (like the persons of the Christian Trinity.)

But the pillar itself may be further clarified. It operates on the same archetypal level as a symbolic tree. The association of a tree with life and growth is universal, from the tree of immortality in the center of Eden to the Norse world-tree Yggdrasil. The *Svipdagsmal* (part of the thirteenth-century Old Norse *Poetic Edda*) says of Yggdrasil:

> "Tell me this, then, Fjolsvid," Svipdag said, "What issues from the seed of this mighty tree that neither axe nor fire will fell?"
>
> "Women in childbirth cook the fruit," said the giant, "Then the hidden child is delivered safely. That's why people esteem it."

A sixth-century BC vase from Boeotia (Hesiod's home) showing Hecate, flanked by lions, with a crown of branches, blessing and protecting two young women.

Another sixth-century BC Hecate, this one from Tenos, an island midway between Greece and Hecate's home in Asia Minor.

A reconstruction of the Tenos Hecate.

The sacred-pole deities I have just mentioned are typically represented as trees as well. The worship of Ashtoreth, interchangeably as a pole-fetish or as a holy tree, is copiously attested in the Bible, where the prophets denounce the practice with monotonous zeal. Similarly, the sycamore tree was equated with Hathor by the Egyptians.

A vase from the sixth century BC showing a figure who may well be Hecate, judging by the flanking lions, and the animals that suggest dominion over sea (fish), land (lions, bull) and air (birds).

We are not then surprised to see that Hecate appears crowned with oak leaves in the surviving fragments of the fifth-century BC Greek playwright Sophocles' *The Witches*, as well as in the *Argonautika*, an epic poem by the third-century BC Greek Apollonius of Rhodes.

It may well be Hecate who, with a crown of branches offers maternal blessing to two maidens who embrace her from either side on a sixth-century BC stamped vase from Boeotia (shown above) — the time and home of Hesiod whose hymn to Hecate we have just seen.

The pair of lions flanking the figure help secure the identification of this image with Hecate. Lions are shown beside Hecate in first century BC on coins and in a temple-frieze from her homeland. Hundreds of years later, in the second to fourth centuries AD *Greek Magical Papyri*, Hecate is still described as accompanied by lions. The lions represent the goddess as nurturer of animal life, and there are a constant in depictions of fertility goddesses (see the figure of the Mycenean pillar goddess from the sixteenth-century BC, above).

To say that Hecate is a fertility goddess often represented by a pole or a tree is no more that to say she is a typical near-eastern fertility goddess, absolutely conventional in form. She is a local Turkish cognate of Ashtoreth, Hathor and the Mycenean goddesses we know from seals and figurines.

It is my contention that Hecate is not only a fertility goddess, a "tree of life." She is also an example of the archetype which historians of religion call the "world-tree." This I deduce from another well-attested feature of her being — her access to many worlds. In his Hecate hymn in *The Theogony*, Hesiod says:

> Zeus gave her splendid gifts:
> a share of the fruitful earth and barren sea
> he gave her a share of starry heaven too,
> there she is honored exceedingly by the deathless gods.

Thus, Hecate participates in the three realms of the Homeric dispensation: those ruled by Zeus, Poseidon and Hades. The hymn continues:

> To this day, whenever any man on earth
> offers rich sacrifices and prays for favor,
> the custom is to call upon Hecate.
> Great honor comes full easily to him
> whose prayers the goddess receives favorably,
> and she bestows wealth upon him too,
> for power surely is with her.

Clearly Hecate, who facilitates prayer, is an intermediary between the world of gods and that of men. This role is corroborated by her appearance as a messenger spirit in a poem by the fifth-century BC poet Pindar; hundreds of years later she still has the same role, when she appears as the *catalyst* of Medea's prayer to Youth in Ovid's *Metamorphoses*.

All ritual trees and posts used in religious ceremonies partake, to some extent, in the character of the Universal Tree which marks the center of the world (e.g., the Kabbalistic Tree of Life, the Germanic *WeltAsche*) whose roots are in hell, whose branches touch heaven — the bridge which makes possible communication between the worlds. In her classic treatment of Haitian Voodoo, *Divine Horsemen*, Maya Deren says of the *poteau mitain* ("center pole") in the midst of the *humfo* (voodoo temple):

> And if one or another tree is particularly consecrated to this *loa* (spirit) or that, it is not because the *loa* is the spirit *of* the tree, it is, rather, in the sense of that tree as a preferred avenue of divine approach. The stylized tree, its branches and roots symmetrically extended to both sides of an horizon, is signaled, over and over in the *vevers* (stylized patterns sacred to individual *loa*). As a center-post — *poteau-mitain* — this same vertical avenue, axis of

117

the metaphysical cosmos, is built into the very center of the *peristyle*, the ceremonial enclosure. Around this *poteau-mitain* revolve the ritual movements and the dance; at its base the offerings are placed; and through it the *loa* enter the peristyle.

Of the sacrificial stake (*yupa*) of Vedic India, the *Satapatha Brahmana* (one of the commentaries on the Vedas written between 900 and 500 AD) says:

> With your summit you hold up the heavens, with your branches you fill the air, with your foot you steady the earth.

To return to Hecate: Her world-tree like communication with all the realms, which explains her role as a facilitator of prayers, is a point very explicitly made by Sophocles in this fragment of his play *The Witches*:

> O Lord Helios!
> O sacred flame of the torch wayfaring Hecate holds by her,
> the torch she carries when she ranges in the realm of Olympus
> and when she returns to the earth, site of the crossroads,
> the crossroads, her sacred place;
> Hecate, crowned with oak and woven coils of fierce serpents . . .

Six hundred years later, the first-century AD Roman epic poet Lucan describes a more demonic Hecate who still has access to all realms. His character, the arch-witch Erictho, says

> Persephone, who is the third and lowest aspect
> of Hecate, the goddess we witches revere,
> Hecate, through whom I can silently converse with the dead . . .

and

You, Hecate, rotting goddess,
with your pallid decaying body, you who have to wear a mask
when you visit the gods in heaven,
obey me or I shall show you to them as you are,
you who look like hell.

Relevant here is Hecate's depiction as gate-guardian, holder of the keys that open the realms. Her earliest inscription (sixth-century BC) calls her protectress of entrances, and *hekataia* would commonly be placed, *mezzuzah*-like, at the doors of palace and private home alike. Thus Hecate opens the adamantine gates of Death in a poem by the third-century BC Greek poet Theocritus, and the entrance to hell is described by the first-century AD Roman poet Vergil as Hecate's grove. There Aeneas enters the world of the dead, invoking Hecate in her role of bridge between the realms,

calling aloud on Hecate, powerful in Heaven and Hell.

At the end of antiquity, in *The Greek Magical Papyri*, Hecate is described over and over as holder of the key of Tartaros, the deepest pit of Hell.

At this point we are equipped to understand some of the attributes of the classical Hecate images I have so far left undiscussed. The long torch she carries when she helps Demeter search for Persephone in the seventh-century B.C. *Hymn to Demeter*, and that we have just seen in the fragment of Sophocles' *The Witches*, probably indicates her role as guide on all journeys, great or small. The libation bowl and ewer would stand for her facilitating prayer at sacrifices, where the pouring of libations was a basic component; the fruit witnesses her fertility function.

As regards Hecate's antiquity, geography, etymology, genealogy and role in esoteric religion, I have merely brought, albeit for the first time, the research of other scholars into one convenient account. The understanding of her depiction as sacred pole, tree of life and world axis is entirely new and constitutes a complete departure from traditional scholarly interpretation.

I will call on one more outside witness: the sacred-pole fertility god of Dahomey, Legba.

According to Dahomean myth, Legba was born to Mawu and Lisa, the twin rulers of the sky, after all the realms had been apportioned. In compensation, Legba was made Mawu and Lisa's representative on all the planes of being. Legba is then, like Hecate, a world-axis type, bridging the realms. He thus becomes an intermediary for all communication with the gods. The mythological explanation is that Mawu and Lisa gave to each god a language that was appropriate to his realm. Legba interprets these different and mutually incomprehensible languages so that god may speak to god, and gods may talk with man. In the classic study *Dahomey, An Ancient African Kingdom*, the Herskovitses relate

> Therefore if any of the children of Mawu-Lisa, on earth or elsewhere, wish to address their parents or each other, they must transmit their messages through Legba, for they can no longer communicate directly. Thus Legba is everywhere; he is found even before the houses of the *vodu* (spirits, deities) themselves, and this is because all living creatures must address themselves to him before they can be understood by the gods.

which calls to mind Hesiod's

To this day, whenever any man on earth
offers rich sacrifices and prays for favor,
the custom is to call upon Hecate.

Brought to Haiti by the slaves, Legba there retains his role, and is the first god saluted in all ceremonies as the one who makes communication between the realms possible. A ritual song of greeting to Legba quoted in Metraux's *Voodoo in Haiti* runs

Atibon-Legba, remove the barrier for me, *agoé* !
Papa Legba remove the barrier
So I may pass through.
When I come back I will salute the *loa*.
Voodoo Legba, remove the barrier for me
So that I may come back;
When I come back, I will thank the *loa*. *Abobo*.

Syncretism with Catholic Saints is standard in Afro-Carribean religion, and Legba is identified with St. Peter — who holds the keys of Heaven and Hell — an association copiously paralleled for Hecate who is called "key-bearer" in the Greek Magical Papyri.

Legba is also a protection-granting fertility god, represented in front of each Dahomean house (like the Greek *hekataion*) by a small earth mound in which is planted a phallic rod of wood or iron. The custom obtains in Haiti as well.

In Dahomey, Legba is the principal god sacrificed to in childbirth and receives signal honor in marriage rites; so too in Haiti, where his childbirth invocation includes (according to the Herkovitses) the phrase:

Open the road for me . . . do not let any evil spirit bar my path.

This recalls Hecate's birth-helper role mentioned in reference to the archaic Artemis.

Finally, the pole which represents the cosmic axis, set up in the center of the Voodoo temple, the *poteau mitain* ("center pole"), is also called the *poteau Legba* ("Legba pole.") Similarly, the pole that stands for Hecate is a *hekataion*.

Queen of Heaven, Queen of Hell

Seal from about the third century AD, showing Hecate with daggers, whips, short torches and snakes. She maintains her triple form and central pillar.

In the sixth book of the Aeneid, Vergil calls Hecate "powerful in heaven and hell alike" — a striking formulation, and a deeply problematic one.

The Hecates of Greek literature are likewise both heavenly and hellish. Hesiod sang of a Hecate who was a fostering all-mother. It was an innocent, nymph-like Hecate who helped search for kidnapped Persephone in the *Hymn to Demeter*. But it was Hecate the queen of hell and mistress of the witches that appeared in Sophocles and Euripides. Yet while Athenian audiences shuddered at these horrific Hecates, they also heard her hymned by Aeschylus as a benign birth-helper, and Phidias' pupil Alcamenes placed her beautiful triple shape at the entrance of the Acropolis. Vergil's line summarizes the contradiction in Hecate, but offers no solution.

In her native Asia Minor, Hecate was venerated alongside the goddess Roma, and later worshiped alongside the deified Caesar — so surely she had to be, like Caesar's wife, "above suspicion." But then how can the poet Horace, in the same period, describe wicked witches invoking Hecate in a cemetery on Rome's Esquiline hill to further their awful magic?

Almost all the statues of Hecate we have are from the fourth to first centuries BC, almost all are from Athens and nearby Attica. But despite this agreement in time and place, they come in two contradictory varieties. In the one case the three figures are ranged around their pillar holding torches long enough to reach the ground. They may also carry ewers and libation bowls and fruit. Dogs sit at their feet. The other series retains the dog but shows figures with short torches, whips, serpents and keys, Hellish indeed!

Classics scholars at the end of the twentieth century declared research at an impasse. They decided that the original nature of Hecate (described in the previous chapter), was forever unknowable. The contradictory holy-infernal later descriptions were incomprehensible. End of discussion.

But about a century ago Ulrich von Wilamowitz-Möllendorff (1848-1931), the greatest classical philologist of all time, resolved the problem of Hecate's dual nature with a few brief and brilliant remarks. (Wilamowitz, by the by, if he is known to non-specialists, is known only because of his withering review of Nietzsche's *Birth of Tragedy*, which made a very hurt Nietzsche abandon the field of classical philology.)

Wilamowitz pointed out that, until the fifth century B.C., no one had anything but good to say of Hecate. But then, said Wilamowitz, judging by the literary and archaeological record, Hecate was, during the fifth century, gradually conflated with the goddess Enodia from Thessaly (northern Greece).

To develop Wilamowitz' insight, we have to took at Enodia in detail. Unfortunately we know little beyond her name. She makes her first appearance in literature with *Helen* by the fifth-century BC playwright Euripides. When Menelaus sees the real Helen in Egypt, he can't believe his eyes. The play has,

> Menelaus: O Hecate, torch bearing night-wanderer, send your visions kindly!
> Helen: You see in me no ghost, no nocturnal servant of Enodia.

Enodia's homeland was Thessaly, where her cult was centered in the city of Pherai. This region was well settled in the neolithic, just like adjacent Asia Minor, and thus fertility goddesses were particularly prominent there as well.

The Euripides passage makes it clear that Enodia has a retinue of ghosts, and this suggests a similar host, the *wütende Heer*, which attends the fertility goddesses (Holda, Berchte, Herodias, Dame Abonde &c.) of European folklore. The Brothers Grimm made a classic study of this folklore motif in chapter thirteen of their *Teutonic Mythology*.

Our richest source of testimony for Enodia is the coinage from her city, Pherai, which happily survives for the entire fifth and fourth centuries BC. This shows a goddess in a myrtle crown, one or two torches in hand, riding a horse. In all, an image that goes well with the idea that she is a goddess who leads a horde of ghosts across the night. Also her name, Enodia, "traveler", would be a good fit.

Whatever Enodia originally was in Thessaly, she appears in Greek literature as just another name for Hecate. Hecate has completely absorbed her. This was easy because Hecate was a fertility goddess with special access to all realms. Enodia was a fertility goddess too, with a special close relationship with roads and travel. Enodia is also the queen of the ghosts, and this is a normal *aspect* of all fertility goddesses. They are identified with the earth, which not only brings forth life but is the home of the buried dead. Hecate undoubtedly already had some of Enodia's spooky associations before she met Enodia, though they do not seem to have been very prominent. When Hecate absorbed Enodia her dark side was emphasized. The placement of Hecate's image at the crossroads must have catalyzed the development of a scarier Hecate.

The crossroads is a site with universal spooky implications. To the religious imagination it can appear not as a random juncture of paths but as a place where roads purposefully converge: in Egyptian such an intersection is basic to the concept of "city." The glyph for city, *neywet*, shows a crossroads. This may help explain the weird feeling associated with a desolate crossroads far from any town — it's like a city center without a city, roads converging on nowhere, or perhaps on the invisible?

A good parallel comes from ancient Japan, where rituals of possession by *Marebito* (gods, god-men, ancestral spirits, souls of the dead), which are the origin of the *No* plays, were performed at the crossroads.

Once the location of the *hekataion* was understood as dark Enodia's sacred site, Hecate drew dark nourishment from the haunted Thessalian plains. Planted in Enodia's home city, Pherai, Hecate went from a tree of life to something approaching a gallows. Thus we have descriptions such as this from Euripides' play *Ion*:

Daughter of Demeter, Enodia, hear,
propitious regent of each public way
Amid the brightness of the day
Nor less when night's dark hour engenders fear . . .

and this from Virgil's Aeneid:

Hecate, whose name is shrieked at night at the crossroads of
cities.

and, by the end of antiquity, *The Greek Magical Papyri* say:

Come, Hecate, goddess
of the crossroads, who with your fire-breathing phantoms
have been allotted dread roads and harsh enchantments . . .

Once she takes on the fatal name Enodia, the torch which
Hecate has carried for at least two hundred years, since the
Hymn to Demeter in the seventh century BC, the torch which
was probably always hers and is her identifying emblem in
art, begins to sputter and smoke, casting lurid light. This
becomes the "gleam of countless torches" that accompanies
her earthquaking manifestation in the third-century BC
Greek poet Apollonius of Rhodes. The first-century AD
Roman philosopher Seneca wrote a play, *Medea*, in which the
title character cries:

My prayers are heard: thrice has bold Hecate bayed loud, and
has raised her accursed fire with its baleful light."

An instructive parallel is provided by the Dahomean
trickster and fertility god Legba. He is represented by a
phallic sacred pole placed in front of every dwelling, very
much like the *hekataion* of classical Athens. He is not, in

Dahomey, particularly associated with the crossroads, which are under the control of the spirit *Aiza*. Legba is deficient in funereal associations in Dahomey, in fact, there a man's relation to his Legba ends with his death, whereupon the Legba-fetish which stood guard before his compound is desacralized and shattered.

When he was brought to Haiti by the slaves, Legba began to be placed at the crossroads. He thus acquired the epithet *Maît' Carrefour* (Lord of the Crossroads) and became a god involved in sorcery — without however forfeiting his other associations. His ambivalent nature and the way it was gained mirrors Hecate's great mother and witch mistress status. The fusions with Enodia brought spooky overtones to the sacred-pole goddess Hecate; she was particularly susceptible to these through her pre-existing connection with the crossroads, especially where three paths met.

Seemingly we have solved the problem of the double Hecate, but in so doing we have raised a new and more troubling question. Enodia *was* a fertility goddess with more pronounced underworld associations than Hecate, but the record of her veneration in Thessaly suggests a character in no way *demonic*. Nor can everything be attributed to the crossroads — Hermes is, after all, a god of the crossroads and a frequent visitor to the world of the dead without forfeiting thereby his bright Homeric character. (Indeed, we might also ask, what was it that happened to Legba between Dahomery and Haiti, that made him take on the traits of a god of sorcery? The crossroads alone would not have been enough.)

We know when Hecate and Enodia fused, and that the result was immediately pronounced infernal by the Greeks, despite the fact that their positive features were preserved alongside and intact — but why? It would seem to argue a profound ambivalence in the Graeco-Roman soul towards something Hecate and Enodia represent. A troubling conundrum, asking of us most delicate further reflection.

Underneath the Moon

"Everything that exists beyond the moon is eternal." — Cicero, The Republic

Back in the nineteenth century, classics scholars relentlessly interpreted all of Hecate's attributes as lunar. Researchers of the present day, though no longer moonstruck, have made no move towards questioning this opinion. But, in fact, Hecate is never identified or even associated with the moon until the Roman period.

Much of the confusion arises from a general failure among classicists to appreciate the very central place of the moon in the Roman religious world. The moon was for the Romans what Eleusis was for the Greeks: the most potent symbol of the everlasting cycles of nature and existence. For the Roman, the waxing, waning, ever self-renewing moon made a promise that all that dies may return to life in season.

The reason Luna's prominent place in Roman religion is so unacknowledged is embarrassingly simple. The Romans learned literature, and indeed literacy, from the Greeks. Accordingly, their intellectual career began as a slavish imitation of Greek models. To some extent, it always remained that.

The Romans expressed their own religious world using Greek mythology, and to such an extent that the world of Roman mythology is almost completely lost. It's quite understandable when we think back to the beginnings of American literature. What American poet of the nineteenth century would have wanted to write a poem about Johnny

Appleseed or Paul Bunyan when he could take as his topic King Arthur or Achilles?

So, books like Ovid's *Metamorphoses*, the first-century AD bible of classical mythology, give the modern reader a rather skewed view of Roman religion. Greek mythology is retold by Roman poets, with here and there a Latin name (Jove for Zeus, Juno for Hera, and so on), but that's about the extent of the Roman content. The Roman authors are not, as a rule, presenting a mythology they shared with the Greeks, but one which they adopted from them. In fact, the respective pantheons and myths of Greece and Rome have as much, and as little, in common as the Greek and Latin languages. The student of Roman mythology has little more to go on than the odd incongruous Roman religious detail thrown into a Greek story. In Latin literature, Greek myth replaced Roman myth even more thoroughly than Christian mythology did the native Celtic and Germanic traditions of Europe.

While the moon stood at the very center of Roman mythology, it was, for the Greeks, a very peripheral figure. The Greeks gave the moon only the minor myths of Selene and Endymion. Thus the literary Romans, determined to be Greek, had no way of talking about the moon. Nevertheless, the truth of their moon-worship keeps peering out from behind the Grecian clouds.

The first-century BC Roman scholar and polymath Varro, at the beginning of his work on agriculture, places the moon among the twelve gods. The first-century AD poet Virgil begins his epic poem about agriculture, the *Georgics*, with an invocation to the moon and stars:

> O moon and stars, the sky's most radiant lights,
> who guide the year smoothly through in it's cycle . . .

— it is only after the moon and her sparkling retinue have been saluted that he addresses the gods Dionysus and Demeter, whom the Greeks considered the deities of agriculture. In the same spirit, the poet Horace, Virgil's friend, writes:

> . . . you sing the praises due to the children of Latona, the sun and the moon, the orb of night, who as her light increases ripens the crops and speeds along months.

As the first-century AD orator Cicero puts it in his book The Gods:

> . . . the moon . . . advances pregnancies and ripens them into births . . .

In fact, the Romans believed the moon affected all earthly developments: wind, rain and tides, human and animal life, even the "growth" of minerals, and earthquakes. But her influence is most strong upon the vegetable kingdom. The second-century AD historian Suetonius says, in a surviving fragment of his book *Nature* :

> The moon is a great magnet for vapor and for all substances characterized by moisture. When the moon grows, so do all fruits, and as it wanes, they shrink too.

There is much specific advice from all the Roman writers on agriculture (of whom there are quite a few!) as to when it is best to plant or harvest the various plants. And all the information is given with reference to the lunar cycle. The Greeks gave no such role to the moon. One example will suffice. The seventh-century BC Greek poet Hesiod, in his poetic handbook on farming, *Works and Days*, reckons the times for planting, harvesting and so on by weather signs, rainfall, bird and plant appearances — to the exclusion of the moon.

The role of the moon in agriculture means something very special in the Roman context. The Romans considered agriculture the finest and most improving of human pursuits, it was the very essence of who they were. Cicero says in his book *Duties*:

> But of all the occupations by which you can earn a living, none is better than agriculture, none more advantageous, none more delightful, none more becoming to a free man.

Every urban Roman's ambition was to someday have enough money to buy a farm and retire to the country. The most characteristic Roman building, the *villa*, is a farmhouse: it isn't designed for a city, but to be a walled compound out in the country. Acquiring territory that would become the empire was the great collective venture of Roman society, and the term the Romans used for their lands was the *ager Romanus*, which means "lands subjected to the Roman plough."

So if the Romans saw the moon as mistress of agriculture, this made her the very heart of their emtire world. So powerful a fertility goddess as the Roman moon would, of course, tend to absorb late-arrived goddesses who shared symbolism with her. So it was with Isis. Introduced into Rome in the early first century AD and extremely popular, she is described in the *The Golden Ass*, a novel by the second-century AD North African Latin author Apuleius. The passage is worth citing in full as it illustrates many of the points I will soon make:

About midnight, when I'd slept for a few hours, I awakened with a start, and saw the moon shining as brightly as when she is full. Suddenly she was there, risen so fast it seemed she had literally leaped out of the sea. Then I thought to myself that now, at the secret midnight hour, was when the moon was at the height of her powers. All human affairs are governed by the moon, as are all animals, tame or wild. All living things are strengthened by her light and divine power, and so are inanimate and lifeless things. Every substance in the heavens, the earth and the seas is increased as she increases, and diminishes as she diminishes.

Weary from all my cruel misfortunes and personal disasters, I conceived the hope that I might yet be rescued by invocation and prayer to this powerful and beautiful goddess. So, shaking off my drowsiness, I arose smiling and, feeling a strong longing to purify myself, I went down to the shore and plunged my head seven times into the water (seven is a holy and divine number, as wise Pythagoras knew). Then awake, alert and glad (though weeping), I made this prayer to the powerful goddess:

"O blessed queen of heaven, should I call you Demeter, the original and motherly fosterer of all growing things in the earth, who, after finding your daughter Persephone, were so joyful that you replaced the original human diet of nuts and berries with something better? You made the barren ground of Eleusis to be ploughed and sown, and provided mankind with better and more delicate foods made from grain. Or shall I call you heavenly Venus, who, at the beginning of the world, joined together male and female in conjugal love for the eternal propagation of humankind? Or shall I call you sister of the god Apollo, the goddess who saves so many people by easing the pangs of childbirth, like a divine physician, the great Diana adored at Ephesus? Or shall I call you terrible Hecate? You terrify with doglike howlings, you with triple face, you who control the hordes of ghosts, who are able to make them appear or keep them hidden in the Earth! You are a goddess who wanders through many groves and sacred places, worshiped in many manners. You illuminate all the cities of the earth by night with your feminine, lunar light; you nourish all the seeds of the world with the warm moisture you create, you whose light changes depending on how the sun's light touches you; I call on you by whatsoever name or shape it is right to call upon you . . .

The goddess who answers this opulent invocation is Isis. She is described with the titles of many deities, but she clearly appears in the form of the moon. This is quite interesting. Isis never possessed lunar features in Egypt. (There *was* an Egyptian moon god, the minor deity Khons.) The specific powers Apuleius attributes to his lunar Isis are precisely those we have seen the Romans attributing to the moon for hundreds of years.

Isis was the major fertility goddess in Egypt. The Roman Apuleius expressed this by describing Isis in terms of the moon, the goddess whom the Romans considered the giver of all fertility. Exactly the same thing will happen with Hecate: because she is a fertility goddess, the Romans feel they are right to make her lunar. When Romans adopt foreign mythologies, they don't always completely replace their own beliefs. They create hybrids, foreign in form but Roman in content — at least when that content is as important to the Roman soul as the moon was.

But while every fertility goddess was compatible with Luna (as Apuleius' prayer makes clear), Hecate had something that guaranteed her complete and lasting synthesis with the Roman moon: the very superficial matter of Hecate's triple form. This was what swung Hecate decisively into a lunar orbit.

The Roman moon was a triple deity, long before she came in contact with Hecate. In fact, she was triple as far back as inscriptions and historical records take us, which is to the sixth century BC Hecate did not even begin to syncretize with the triple Roman moon goddess before the last quarter of the first century BC, so she couldn't have influenced the Roman moon's depiction.

Before I start marshaling my evidence, I should stress that it's going to look a little patchy. This is because the Romans tended to write about Greek myths and practices, rather than their own, so there isn't that much there. I will piece together the facts from a coin, an inscription, a line from a poet, because there is no surviving text in which a Roman author describes his own religion systematically and in detail. The closest we have to such a deliberate account are the "refutations" of Roman paganism written by early Church fathers.

My method has, however, this advantage: I am using actual Roman evidence to describe Roman religion, instead of assuming, as most classicists do, that there is no important difference between Roman and Greek mythology and religious practice.

At this point we need to start using the name for the moon goddess that the Romans themselves used: Juno. Juno, whose maternal character is anciently and consistently attested, is the most logical representative for the moon as the Romans conceived it. Although we don't have any clear etymology for the name Juno, her constant epithet *Lucina* clearly refers to light (in Latin, *lux*). We may reasonably translate the name Lucina as "luminous." Ovid, in his book *The Calendar*, offers these suggestions as to how we should understand Lucina:

> Ten times the moon had regrown her crescent horns,
> then every husband became a father,

each wife a mother. The curse of infertility was gone
thanks to Juno, whom we call Lucina —
a name which suggests the sacred groves (*lucus*) of the goddess,
and also the fact that you, Juno, are a source of light (*lux*).
Gracious Juno-Lucina, be compassionate to women with child,
gently deliver the womb's ripe burden.

Ovid's suggestion that the name Lucina relates to the word for grove is of course wrong — the ancients had only the vaguest idea of how etymology worked. For them, a pun was as good as a proof. But Ovid is quite correct in his second suggestion, that Lucina comes from the word for light.

Another and stronger piece of evidence for an always lunar Juno comes from the Roman calendar itself. The *Calends*, the appearance of new moon which marked the beginning of the Roman month, were always sacred to Juno. Juno was then equated with the moon by the Romans as far back as they could tell time and reckon dates.

It remains to show that Juno was always triple. Juno bears three names in inscriptions from the cities of Latium (the oldest Roman region in Italy), particularly Lanuvium, where we find inscriptions to *Iunone seispiti matri reginae*, that is, "Juno: Defender, Mother, Queen." To understand the meaning of these three titles, we need to use the discoveries of Georges Dumezil. His great works proved the survival of pan-Indo-European beliefs and attitudes among the peoples who descended from them, most notably in the tripartite division of society into Royal-Priestly, Warrior, and Agricultural classes. The Hindu *Brahman*, *Kshatriya* and *Vaisya* castes are the parade example of this.

Triple Juno from a first-century BC Roman coin.

In his book *Archaic Roman Religion* Dumezil interprets this inscription as testimony to Juno's involvement in the Warrior ("Defender,") Agricultural ("Mother") and Royal-Priestly ("Queen") segments of society.

Other evidence for a triple Juno comes from a first-century BC Roman coin (shown above) which has three female figures with linked arms, the one on the left holding a bow, that on the right a poppy. Behind them are cypress trees. There is also a horizontal bar behind them, and this is a visual convention to show that the figures are to be understood as inseparable. Such a bar is used, for example, in depictions of the twin gods Castor and Pollux. The image bears no name, but provides a remarkable parallel to the triple Juno of the Dumezilian inscriptions. We see bow-bearing Diana on the left for Juno the "Defender;" Proserpine, with her traditional poppy, on the right for the agricultural "Mother;" Juno Lucina, the essence of the whole conception, in the very center as befits the "Queen."

This threefold Roman Juno attested to by the earliest Roman inscriptions and early Roman coins was triple, but not in the way that Hecate was. She was part of a trio of deities who were seen as being, at the same time, one and separate. She was a real trinity in the Christian sense. And the members of this trinity were, the Roman poets tell us, Juno, Diana and Proserpine.

Let us now turning to the other members of the Juno triad, Diana was a goddess originally from Latium, in central Italy (the place of the inscriptions), with a major sanctuary in the Alban hills close to Rome. In her shrine there, in a wood on the shore of a mountain lake, she was served by a priest known as *Rex Nemorensis*, "the woodland king." This was a slave or fugitive who could be replaced as monarch of the forest by anyone who killed him. There is too little information to truly clarify these tantalizing details. Sir George Frazer wrote his *Golden Bough*, an encyclopedia of comparative anthropology, in a quixotic attempt to understand the *Rex Nemorensis*. The preface and conclusion of his book, which give his results, are still worth reading, both as a daring reconstruction of the rites, and for Frazer's own deliciously lurid musings and tumescent prose.

Diana was understood by the Romans as their version of the Greek virgin huntress Artemis, and in the literary and artistic record the Latin deity is pretty much lost under the Greek overlay. But two essential details emerge. Diana, like Artemis, carries a bow, she's an *armed* goddess, and second, she's consistently listed as an aspect of a triple fertility goddess. This strongly supports the theory that she is the warrior aspect of a Dumezilian Indo-European triad. A good look at the Roman Diana is provided by this poem by Horace, who describes her as a forest goddess to whom the spoils of the hunt are sacrificed.

> O maiden goddess, guardian of hill and grove,
> you that, thrice invoked, hear the cries
> of young mothers in childbirth pangs
> and rescue them from death, goddess of the triple form,
> I dedicate to you this pine tree towering over my home.
> Here I shall gladly sacrifice to you
> each year, a young boar just learning how to slash
> with a sidelong thrust of the tusk.

The third part of the trinity is Persephone (Proserpine in the Roman spelling), the Greek goddess of agriculture whom the Romans used to represent their own agriculture goddess Ceres. Again, the replacement is so complete that all that remains which we can securely call Roman is her agricultural role, and her description as part of the Juno-trinity. The literary record for Roman Proserpine is so sparse that we cannot do better than to cite her appearance in a poem by the Roman poet Catullus, which gives us the fullest description of the Juno trinity we possess:

> Under Diana's protection, pure girls and virgin boys,
> we sing of Diana, daughter of Leto, high powerful child of
>   universal Jove,
> born beside an olive tree on Delos,
> huntress, lady of the mountains,
> lady of the moist fresh forest,
> lady of secret valleys and loud fast rivers.
> Diana whose name is Lucina, Lightbringer,
> who every month restores the vanished moon,
> Diana whose name is Juno Lucina,

who hears the pained prayers of birthing women.
Diana whose name is Trivia —
the crossroads her sacred place —
night goddess, queen of the underworld.

Threefold Diana, huntress, birth-helper,
and Luna shining with borrowed light.
Diana, in your monthly circle
measuring out the turning year,
filling the farmer's rough-walled barn
with fruit and produce, vegetables and grain.
Be you holy and exalted by whatever name will please you!
and now, as of old, with your good power,
protect the people of Romulus.

Catullus describes the trinity in terms of Diana (Juno's warrior aspect), Juno Lucina, and Proserpine (whom the poet here calls Trivia). Catullus has given us the same image we find on the coin discussed above.

I think we should regard the synthesis of Diana and Proserpine with Juno as *Juno influencing Diana and Proserpine*. Only Juno is early and clearly documented as a triple goddess in archaic inscriptions from Latium, and Juno has an widespread prestige and a lunar meaning that old Roman Diana and Proserpine never did.

Catullus' use of the name Trivia for Proserpine is, of course, a reference to Hecate (it's a Latin epithet made directly from the Greek word for crossroads, *triodos*). Catullus uses the associations of the name Trivia to emphasize the underworld aspect of Proserpine who, though primarily the goddess of the planted seeds, is also queen of all else that's buried.

This use of the epithet Trivia is the first time that Hecate herself, albeit indirectly, appears in Roman literature. From the start, Hecate is virtually submerged in the Latin and lunar triple deity. Of the Greek Hecate there survives in the Roman record at most an epithet or a descriptive detail, like an extinguished torch bobbing unhappily on the Luna-ruled waves. (This does not really contradict my earlier statements that Roman religion was nearly lost under the inundation of Greek influence. The Roman cosmos resists and remains *only in a case like that of the moon,* which was at the very heart of their religious world.)

The Greek Hecate herself never had lunar traits, nor was she understood in Greece as a corporate entity comprised of three separate goddesses. Her introduction to Rome brought about these profound changes.

One further metamorphosis awaited Hecate eclipsed by the moon: reformulation in philosophical terms. From the second to fourth centuries AD, while Greek rationalism finally came to terms with Greek religiosity, popular systems of belief arose that offered syntheses of philosophy and mysticism. The *Chaldean Oracles* are a very sophisticated example of the trend, *The Greek Magical Papyri* a fairly vulgar one.

In the *Magical Papyri* Hecate has gone beyond being a fertility goddess, one who supervises the cycle of organic growth, decay and rebirth. Now she is not the producer of change but Change itself — which the Greeks considered the essence of what was wrong with the world of matter. Change entails decay, and growth itself is thus a kind of death-sentence. The entire conception is given in the *Magical Papyri* with impressive continuity. On the one hand Hecate is the mother of all growth:

> . . . Hecate, Mistress
> of night and underground realms, holy, black-clad,
> you are the moon that waxes till it tugs

at the world revolving in space among the stars.
It is you who produced every physical thing,
you engendered everything on earth,
everything in the sea, and all the different races
of flying, nesting birds.
Mother of all, who gave birth to Cupid, you are Aphrodite,
and the lamp-bearer Selene, shining and aglow.

Another spell from the *Magical Papyri* states that Lunar Hecate, waxing and waning, provides the pattern of all becoming:

> I call upon you who have all forms and many names, double-horned goddess, Moon, whose form no one knows except him who made the entire world, Jahweh, the one who shaped you into the twenty-eight shapes you assume in the lunar month, which produced all the forms in the world. Through you every creature takes form, through you breath and life come to every animal and plant, so that they flourish, like you who grow from obscurity into light, like you who also finally wane and leave light for darkness.

Hecate is not only identified with Change, but with Chance. She is called "swift *Tyche* (random luck) of daimons and gods" and "Selene, only Ruler, the Fortune of daimons and gods." The *Magical Papyri* go on to call her the random Chance which is stronger than Providence:

> Hail, Holy Light, Ruler of Tartaros,
> who strike with rays; hail, Holy Beam, who whirl
> up out of darkness and subvert all things
> with aimless plans. I'll call and may you hear
> my holy words since awesome Destiny
> is ever subject to you.

The association which went from Growth to Change to Chance ends with Doom:

... you're Justice and the Moira's (Fate's) threads:
Klotho and Lachesis and Atropos
(the goddesses who weave Fate into being) ...

From the fates to the furies, (the spirits who bring death and punishment to the wicked,) the transition is easy:

Necessity
hard to escape are you; you're Destiny and
the fury Erinys, Torment, Justice and Destroyer,
you keep Cerberus in chains, with scales
of serpents are you dark, O you with hair
of serpents, serpent-girded, who drink blood ...

But both Growth and Decay, Creation and Doom, are encompassed by the cosmic and complete lunar Hecate:

Beginning
and end are you, and you alone rule all,
for all things are from you, and in you do all things, eternal one,
come to their end.

A Howling at the Gate

The accounts of Hecate as the goddess of the witches, all literary, only begin in the fifth century BC, 200 years after a completely un-demonic Hecate was introduced into the Olympian family and Greek literature by Hesiod. My task here shall be to demonstrate that the Hecate of the witches is not a suppressed aspect of the goddess, but the result of a long a methodical, albeit unconscious, demonization of her benign and ordinary traits.

The actual rites and practices associated with Hecate are reliably attested to only by inscriptions, and the tid-bits of social history one finds in the comic authors and antiquarians. We can trust this material because there is no motive for falsification. We can probably assume that whatever we have attested for in this manner is true for a few hundred years back as well: religion tends to be rather conservative, and typically preserves wording, dress and ritual even after the original meaning has long been forgotten.

Perhaps the best testimony to Hecate's original rites are the inscriptions from the Lagina temple in her Asia Minor homeland, dating from the fourth to second centuries BC. These mention eunuch priests — a commonplace for the great goddesses of Asia Minor — and the mysterious office of "key-bearer," apparently filled by a priestess who carried a key in some sacred procession. This constitutes virtually our entire fund of information on her native rites, but is happily paralleled by the earliest (sixth-century BC) inscription for Hecate's cult in Greece — on an altar in the temple of Apollo Delphinius at Miletus, where she shares with him the title "protector of entrances."

In Greece Hecate was regarded as a universal door-warder and gate-guardian, and so stood before palaces, temples and all private homes. A character in Aristophanes' play *The Wasps* says:

> You see, the oracles are coming true: I have heard it foretold that one day the Athenians would dispense justice in their own houses, that each citizen would have himself a little tribunal constructed on his porch, just like the Hecate-fetishes they have at every door.

The pole-like Hecate-fetish (*hekataion*, plural: *hekataia*) was regarded as conferring a general protection on all who dwelt within a house or passed through its doors. An ancient commentary on the Aristophanes' play says:

> *Hekataion*: Hecate-fetish: the Athenians set her up everywhere as guardian and child-nurturer.

This good influence seems to have extended to travel as well. Various sorts of fortune-telling were routinely performed by the priests at pagan temples: Hecate was consulted (through an oracular priest) before taking a trip. Aristophanes has a character in his play *Lysistrata* say:

> Theagenes' wife is sure to come at any rate; she has actually been to consult Hecate.

Likewise, a safe return was an occasion for giving Hecate thanks. Among the many inscriptions included in *The Greek Anthology* (a sort of ancient *Norton Anthology* which continued to be re-edited and expanded from the first century BC to the tenth century AD), is this one to Hecate:

Hecate, goddess of travelers,
Antiphilus dedicates to you this hat
that protected his head all through his journey,
because you heard his supplication and blessed his path.
The gift is not great, but given with pious awe.
May greedy travelers think twice about snatching away my
     offering:
It is not safe to steal even little gifts from a shrine.

However, Hecate's association with travel, exits and entrances had become demonic by the third century BC. A poem from this period by Theocritus depicts an amateur sorceress who invokes Hecate saying:

O Hecate, just as you can open the steel door of Death,
so you can move all else that is is unshakable.
Listen, Thestylis, the dogs howl in town,
Hecate is surely appearing at the crossroads.

As late as second to fourth centuries AD *Greek Magical Papyri*, Hecate is conjured up on a night "in which the bar of Hell-gate is opened" and addressed by a magician who says: "I . . . posess your key. I opened the door of Hell, the door Cerberus guards . . . " Elsewhere in the *Magical Papyri* she is invoked in the name of her key and thrice-locked door and called ". . . you who've opened the gates of steel unbreakable," "gate-breaker," and quite simply "key."

Another of Hecate's standard roles seems to have been to receive remnants of household propitiatory and purification offerings, as well as the sweepings from ritual housecleaning, that were burned before the Hecate-fetish of the crossroads or the doorway. The potsherd on which the rubbish was burnt was carried away, thrown, and abandoned without looking back. The Greek playwright Aeschylus has a character in *The Libation Bearers* say,

> Or shall I pour this libation on the ground, for Earth to drink,
> without a word, without respect,
> the way my father was slain and left to lie?
> Shall I go home without a single backward glance,
> just throw away the libation bowl, as if I were flinging
> out, on the public road, for Hecate,
> the dirt from a ritual housecleaning?

The purpose of the ritual housecleaning was the removal of earthy substances inimical to the veneration of the celestial Olympian deities. Hecate's custody of rubbish, dirt and uncleanness, a natural and minor specialty for an earth and fertility goddess, reappears in the *Magical Papyri* bizarrely emphasized. Her original positive, if undignified, relation to earthy substances has been perverted into a negative theophany. Now Hecate is called *Borborophorba*, "the Eater of Filth." She takes her dinner in the graveyard, a characterization which is unpleasantly developed in:

> O nether and nocturnal and infernal
> goddess of dark, grimly, silently
> munching the dead,
> Night, Darkness, broad Chaos, you're Necessity,
> hard to escape are you: you're Moira and
> Erinys, Torment, Justice and Destroyer,
> and you keep Cerberos in chains.
> Serpent-scaled, you are dark, with hair
> made of snakes, serpent-girdled, you drink blood,
> you bring death and destruction, you feast
> on hearts, flesh eater, you devour those untimely
> dead and you make lamentations ring out . . .

By the epithets Necessity, Justice &c. it becomes clear that Hecate is equated not only with earth, but with all that earth implies: material existence, which carries an implicit death sentence for all that come into being. So profound is Hecate's dirt theophany that it extends to the cosmic limit of Greek philosophical pessimism!

According to the *Magical Papyri*, this rotten Hecate can be simply and respectfully regaled with cow-dung incense, but in special cases one prepares for her a perfume of goat-fat, baboon-excrement, garlic and the like — a concoction so noxious that it is an effective curse to accuse someone else of having prepared it! Strong smells, such as are associated with decay, now constitute the ambiance of earthy-dirty Hecate.

Another reflection of this developed dirt-sacrality is to be found in *The Sacred Disease*, a treatise on epilepsy by the fourth-century BC Greek physician Hippocrates. This states that Hecate is responsible for people defecating on themselves during a seizure. Since the other symptoms reflect the nature or associations of various gods (e.g., if the patient foams at the mouth and kicks, that's due to the war god Ares), we must understand the stink of excrement as Hecate's calling card.

Ecstasy was also part of the piety associated with Hecate — as it was with all the agricultural great goddesses. The Roman goddess Ceres was a sender of madness, as were her ghostly attendants, the *Larvae*. Cybele, Hecate's sister goddess from Asia Minor, had rites so frenzied the Greeks never let her into their pantheon. Apuleius gives us a detailed description of Cybele's services, which included cross-dressing, shouting, dancing, wild music of drums and oboes, self-whipping and wounding, and a trance from which the priest returned with messages from the goddess.

Hecate appears in two fifth-century BC lists of powers associated with frenzy, both of which include Cybele. One is in the aforementioned *The Sacred Disease*. This list makes Hecate's onslaught responsible for madness and for night-terrors that hurl one out of bed. The second passage, from *Hippolytus* by the fifth-century BC Greek playwright Euripides, is worth citing in full:

> Maiden, you must be possessed,
> made crazy by Pan
> or by Hecate, or by the scary Corybantes
> with Cybele the mountain mother!

Finally, Hecate is precisely invoked in the *Magical Papyri* as a sender of "painful frenzy." Sending mental distress to harry and madden various recalcitrant love-objects is her primary task throughout these spells.

The witches, like Hecate, are steeped in ecstasy and madness. The Roman poets of the first-century AD, Horace, Tibullus, Virgil, Ovid, and even the moral philosopher Seneca, are unanimous and detailed on this point. The witches' charms "set the heart ablaze" and "rend the head asunder;" they can "send a man shrieking across the countryside." The witches themselves sport the disheveled, snake-entwined hair of bacchantes — hair which can stand out like the bristles on a boar or a sea-urchin. And like the bacchantes, the witches tear apart live animals with their teeth. The parade example is Medea in Seneca's play of that name, "given to raving" and "staggering, stunned by ecstasy." This Medea invokes Hecate in a manner suggesting the priests of Cybele,

... for you, with bared breast, will I, like a maenad,
smite my arms with the sacrificial knife.
Let my blood flow on the altars!
Accustom yourself, my hand, to draw the sword
and endure the sight of beloved blood.
Self-wounded have I poured forth the sacred stream
that flows through my veins . . ..

Hecate received a wide variety of offerings, bread, and sometimes eels or mullet, and often dog meat The monthly presentation of food to her was called "Hecate's Supper."

An ancient commentary on the playwright Aristophanes' *Plutus* says,

> At the new moon, the first of the month, at evening, the rich sent a meal to Hecate as an offering to the goddess of the crossroads. The poor showed up ravenous, ate the things and claimed that Hecate had devoured them . . . there is a variant tradition that there was no theft involved, but instead deliberate charity. It was usual for wealthy persons to leave a loaf of wheat bread for Hecate and for the poor to take these, as beggars live on sacred offerings.

While dog-sacrifices are not recorded for the original Hecate in Asia Minor, they are abundantly documented for the Greek world — and not only for Hecate. The Greeks considered dog a perfectly ordinary if inexpensive meat. The dog was, like the pig, the customary animal for purification sacrifices, probably due to the frequency of such offerings and the cheapness of the animals. This prosaic rationale for sacrificing dogs to the goddess, and the relatively late association of the dog with Hecate in art and literature, in no way prepares us for the canine's spectacular career in her company.

To be sure, the dog, which appears at the edge of settlements at nightfall, howling mournfully, has often been associated with the moon and death. Also, it frequently bays its warning before danger is visible to the human eye — leading to the reflection that it sees what humans cannot, that is, the spirit world. Thus the dog, unlike Telemachos, recognizes the disguised Athena in Homer's *Odyssey*. The dog's immemorial bad reputation as an eater of corpses, memorialized in the opening lines of the *Iliad*, and its predilection for garbage and excrement, further involves it in the earthy-dirty side of things.

Because the dog had spooky potential, when Hecate was demonized, the dog of her sacrifices was as well. Dog-howls greeted Hecate's manifestation at the crossroads in the Theocritus poem cited above. Theocritus' contemporary Apollonius of Rhodes also has Hecate appear to a fanfare of howls. In fact, in his epic poem, *The Argonautica*, Medea, the priestess of Hecate, dispatches "the Death-spirits, devourers of life, the swift hounds of Hades, who, hovering through all the air, swoop down on the living."

The Roman poet Horace also has hell hounds appear when the witches begin their invocations in a cemetery on Rome's Esquiline.

In the *Magical Papyri* we can observe traces of Hecate's gradual assimilation to her pet. Regarding the company she keeps, she is called "dog-lover," "queen of dogs," and "leader of dog-packs." She is invoked "while dogs howl and will not shut up," has herself "a voice like a dog's bark," and is heard "howling like a dog." Finally, Hecate's doggishness extends to her person, for she is "the dog who can assume the shape of a maiden," and simply "black dog." The ultimate extension of this is the fusion of the dog with Hecate's cosmic persona, which results in a howl that shakes the universe,

154

I offer you this spice, O child of Zeus,
Dart-shooter, Hecate called Artemis, Persephone,
shooter of deer, night-shining, triple-sounding
triple-voiced, triple-headed, Selene,
triple-pointed, triple-faced, triple-necked,
and goddess of the crossroads, you who hold
untiring fire in triple baskets,
you who frequent the crossroads
and rule the thrice-ten days of the lunar month
with your three forms and flames and dogs!
From tuneless throats you send
a dread sharp cry, O goddess,
you raise an awful sound with triple mouths.
Hearing your cry, all worldly things are shaken:
the nether gates and Lethe's holy water
and primal chaos and the gleaming chasm
of Tartaros. At it every mortal thing
and every mortal man, the star-touching mountains,
valleys and every tree and roaring river
and even the restless sea, the lonely echo
and daimons through the world — all shudder at you,
O blessed one, when they hear your dread voice.

We have seen that the *actual veneration* of Hecate provided, at best, cosmetic details or distant inspiration for the much later Hecate of the witches. Earthy associations, the crossroads, ecstasy and hounds reappear in the witch literature in ways that disregard or demonize their original meaning. It's exactly like the relation of actual Voodoo or Santeria — West African paganism syncretized with Roman Catholicism — to the "satanic cults" of tabloids and films.

Hecate was venerated in Greece from Hesiod's time (the seventh-century BC), but it is another two hundred years before a demonic Hecate appears (in the fifth century BC) on the Greek stage in Sophocles' play *The Witches*. The only witches we have record of appear in literary creations. Did they really exist?

The only real *evidence* of classical witchcraft, comes with *The Greek Magical Papyri*, which date from the second to fourth centuries AD. Though the magic there looks a lot like the made-up magic we saw in the earlier, classical literature, it is only based on it — to the extent of actually quoting some of it!

Roman law shares our skepticism regarding the reality of demonic Hecate and the witches: it does not take the witch seriously as a category of criminal. Though poisoning and malefic magic were certainly actionable, the term "witch" never had more than a general and metaphoric status in the Latin language, i.e., it was treated as a myth and figure of speech, just as we might apply the term "Bluebeard" to a class of murderer.

Indeed, we are driven to the novel conclusion that actual witchcraft finally developed *as a result* of the literary mythology. But whence this mythology? The ascertainable details of Hecate veneration didn't produce it. The skewed and tenuous connection of the facts to the fancy suggests rather that the former were *picked over* for spicy details. But why? What *did* the Greco-Roman world hear howling at the barred gate of its awareness, which it was at such pains to explain as the hounds of Hecate?

Part Two
The Witch

Descent of the Goddess

From the summits of heaven
    she looked into the pit,
she was a goddess on the summits of heaven
    but her heart was in hell.
O Inanna, on the summits,
    your heart in hell!

This lady left earth and heaven
    and went down into the pit.

— *Inanna's Journey to Hell*

The first of the Greek witches is Circe, who appears in *The Odyssey*. This Circe is not a witch or even a follower of Hecate; she is herself a goddess (the exact word is *theos*). A century later, Hesiod concurs. In his *Theogony*, Hesiod makes Circe the daughter of Perseis (a sea nymph) and Helios (a sun god). Impeccable credentials of immortal status.

The Homeric Circe's erotic power is no less certain. In *The Odyssey* she has enough confidence in it to attempt to seduce Odysseus even though he has just caught her attempting to turn him into a beast!

Circe pretty much disappears from classical literature, except as an allusion, after Homer, but her place as arch-sorceress is immediately taken over by her niece Medea. Yet Medea, despite a pure descent from gods and nymphs, is not a goddess but a hero. The fifth-century BC Greek poet Pindar describes her in his *Fourth Pythian Ode* as one able to utter immortal prophecies, but that's as godlike as she gets. And not only has Medea lost her aunt's immortality, she's famous, not for seducing, but for being lovestruck. Admittedly Aphrodite has to bring down a special love charm from heaven so Jason can make Medea love him. But the alteration we see from Circe to Medea, the change from inspirer to victim of passion, is a trend that is not reversed by any of the succeeding witches.

Less than twenty lines survive of Sophocles' play *The Witches*, but these show a Medea by moonlight, howling as she harvests deadly magic herbs, a Hecate of the crossroads crowned with infernal serpents, and a Jason who melts wax love-dolls to madden Medea with passion. Medea has now descended so far towards mortal status that she is susceptible to the influence of a voodoo doll — surely a step down from Aphrodite's charm in the Pindar! A lower magic to prevail upon a lesser Medea.

Though Sophocles' witch play is lost, we have a complete Medea from his artistic rival Euripides. This is the most fully and complexly *human* of all the Medeas and, from the point of view of the witch's morphology, we are clearly a step downwards from the heroic ambiance of Pindar, or even the high melodrama of Sophocles' creation. This is a Medea presented with unheroic realism, and the sensuality that is basic to the witch has gone from Pindar's divinely contrived passion, and the potion-motivation of Sophocles' Grecian *gris-gris*, to something closer to the animal or the elemental than the human. This is the Medea who gets back at her ex by murdering all her children by him. This Medea is not merely ruled by her passions, she is tyrannized by them to insanity.

With the witches of the fourth to second centuries BC we begin to find oddly inconsistent accounts. One such is the Medea of Apollonius of Rhodes' *Argonautica*; part innocent girl, part fierce demanding woman. She is described as a demure priestess of Hecate — but of a Hecate who later appears in ghastly nocturnal theophany, hell-hounds and all. Emblematic is Apollonius' description of Medea on her way to the temple of her goddess, which presents a curious mixture of the maidenly and the frightful. Surrounded by her girl attendants, she keeps tucked in her belt infernal concoctions, while her flashing glance, sign of descent from Helios, is shunned by the townspeople as though it were the evil eye.

The ambivalence is personified when a distinction is made between Medea and the other witches:

> . . . for well she knew the way, having often before
> wandered there among the graves
> and among the tough roots, just like the witches.

— a distinction that will be maintained through further witch depictions: the witch is variously old and hideous or young and attractive. What may be the meaning of this schizophrenic depiction — the young witches who radiate the sensual splendor of a fertility goddess, and the crones who appear like a horrid gnostic emblem of the price of generated existence, age and death — I cannot yet address. It must suffice to note the bifurcation and monitor its progress.

Apollonius' complex Medea is less divine (and more infernal) than that of Euripides, while her subjection to love is so great that she served as model for the over-the-top, melodramatic and campy Dido of Vergil's *Aeneid*. Interestingly, Apollonius also shows us a Circe who has retreated from divinity.

This Circe helps Medea and Jason, but not with some supernatural action: she simply performs a purification ritual on their behalf. The great example of her magic power, the turning of men into animals related in the Odyssey, is presented so diffidently that without a previous knowledge of Homer one would never guess her entourage of animals are transformed men.

Apollonius shows us a Circe very humanly tormented by nightmares that suggest Medea's future crime and bloodguilt:

> . . . the hideous remembrance of her dreams
> entered Circe's mind as she pondered.
> She longed to hear the voice of the maiden Medea,
> to speak with her. As soon as Medea raised her eyes from the
>   ground
> and met Circe's gaze, Circe had to tell her.
> All those who were, like Circe and Medea, descendants of
>   Helios,
> were easy to recognize: their eyes flashed
> and gleamed like polished gold when they caught the light.

So runs the description of Circe's interview with her niece Medea. For us, it is a picture with a special poignance, for we can perceive here, in the vestigial feature of the golden glance, the last sunsetting gleam of the witches' vanishing divinity.

Theocritus, writing at the same time as Apollonius, gives us an account of contemporary witchcraft. He tells the story of Simaitha, a young woman in "modern" fourth-century BC Alexandria, who has turned to magic to recapture the affection of a man who has lost interest. Describing her plight and search for a remedy she says,

> Who didn't I approach? The house of what old woman
> who knows how to sing charms did I leave unvisited?

and again, at the conclusion of the poem:

Now I shall bind him in love to me with my magic,
but if he still causes me to suffer,
then, so help me Fate, he shall be found knocking
at the gate of Death. For I tell thee, O Moon,
I have in my cabinet poisons evil enough,
that a woman from Assyria told me how to make.

Simaitha presents a further stage in the transition from goddess to mortal. While Euripides' and Apollonius' Medeas were fully human, they were still heroic figures. Simaitha is all too human; in fact, she is weak. The transition from inspirer of passion to passion's victim is also here; even her determination to make use of poison if all else fails is more a sign of passive frustration than of active rage. A final important point is the splitting of the witch figure into, on the one hand, the lovely girl Simaitha, and on the other, the poison-vending old women who are the more practiced witches. We already saw this in Apollonius. In Roman literature the two complementary figures will be fully realized.

Witches, and indeed magic, are all but absent from early Roman literature; the first surviving Latin treatment of a scene of magic is Virgil's eighth *Bucolic*, from 39 BC, a poem written in evident imitation of several of Theocritus' compositions, especially the Simaitha one cited above. Magic and witches emerge in Latin literature as a part of the wholesale Roman imitation of later Greek literature, and are from the outset very derivative productions.

Thus the heroic Dido of Virgil's *Aeneid*, or the Medea we see in *The Metamorphoses* by his contemporary Ovid, do not undermine our argument that the witch figure is steadily degenerating. Both Virgil and Ovid are consciously imitating elements of the epic style of Apollonius of Rhodes, and so they produce witches who are essentially the same sentimental-heroic type. Likewise we discount, and in fact omit from consideration, the play *Medea* by the first-century AD philosopher Seneca, which is a deliberate imitation of the Medeas of fifth-century BC Greek tragedy. We cannot be fairly expected to take as documents in the witches' ongoing morphology the figures produced by writers who are consciously imitating models up to 600 years old!

With the above exceptions, all the Latin witches take up the new style developed by Theocritus and push forward the tendencies he advanced. The first of these is the early first-century AD poet Horace' witch Canidia.

By now the witch's growing subjection to passion produces a monster of sexual appetite, and the "lewd hag," as Horace calls her, makes her appearance. Canidia, despite her years, is "every sailor's and peddler's girlfriend." Horace even calls Medea, whose impeccable Greek literary credentials prevented truly scurrilous treatment, "the slut from the Black Sea shore." That libertine behavior is now a standard feature of witch activity is revealed by Canidia's rhetorical query:

> Shall I let you laugh safely at having divulged
> the rites of witchery and its orgies
> where Cupid is allowed free range?

The appetites of these abandoned harridans leap the boundaries of nature itself. Canidia's comrade in harms, Folia, is described as having "a man's sexual desires", i.e., she is a lesbian.

Canidia and her friends are "hags." They no longer possess their own teeth or hair. The witch is becoming an ultra of undivine status, an overdue bill of mortality. The long descent form godhood is nearing its conclusion.

The mid first-century AD poet Lucan wrote a wonderfully bizarre historical epic about the Roman civil war. There, witch-sensuality, already developed into a dominant and sadistic type in Horace, disappears into cannibalism. Though he avoids all mention of sex, as befits a prim stoic poet, we find in his witch Erictho a sublimation of witchly eroticism. She culls corpse clippings with her mouth, explicitly as a violent extension of a kiss:

> Often too when a kinsman is buried,
> the dreadful witch hangs over the loved body:
> while kissing it she mutilates the head.
> She forces open the closed mouth
> then, biting the tip of the motionless tongue,
> she pours inarticulate sound into the cold lips
> and sends a message of mysterious horror
> down to the ghosts in hell.

As for mortality, Erictho is beyond that: she lives in a sepulchre which is nothing less than Hell's embassy — an officially recognized outpost of the land of the dead.

In his second-century AD Latin novel *The Golden Ass*, Apuleius creates the witch Meroe, a creature whose lust is so great it cannot be described in physiological terms alone — its range is geographical, as her runaway sex-slave Socrates recounts:

> Then he answered: "Would you like to hear one or two, (or maybe more) of her acts? She forces the people of Thessaly to rage with love for her, and not only them, but even the far off Indians and Ethiopians. And that exercise of her will is just a trifle and taste of her witchly work . . .

Meroe's activities are characteristic of the other Thessalian witches we meet in the opening chapters of the novel. When the hero Lucius' friend Byrrhaena warns him against his hostess, she tells him:

> . . . beware I say, beware of the evil arts and wicked allurements of the Pamphile that is the wife of Milo, whom you call your host, for she is considered the greatest magician and enchantress, mistress of every necromantic spell. By breathing certain words and charms over boughs and stones and other trivial things, she can throw down all the stars into the deep bottom of hell, and reduce them again to primaeval chaos. As soon as she sees any good-looking young man, she is immediately smitten with love for him, and then she can't take her eyes, or her affections, off him. She beguiles a young man's spirit with flattery and catches him in the snares of her limitless lust. Any man who won't give in to her filthy desires she immediately hates and turns into stones or sheep, or whatever beast she pleases, or else she just murders them.

Now there is nothing to suggest any of Apuleius' witches are hags — which presents us with a problem — how do we explain the fact that the last great witches of antiquity revert to an earlier condition of youthful attractiveness? Certainly as regards inversion of sensuality, the movement is still clear and uninterrupted: the witch has, in this regard, gone from planet Venus to Black Hole.

We may understand the survival of the beautiful Apuleian witch alongside the Lucanic hag as the ultimate development of the same ambivalence which produced a similar double witch-image in Theocritus and Apollonius of Rhodes. A substantiation of this is the fact that the tensions that produce on the one hand Erictho and on the other Meroe are to be observed *within* each as well. I have already noted the sensuality submerged in Erictho's cannibalism, it only remains to demonstrate the flesh-dread in Apuleius' seemingly pleasant production. It should suffice to recall that the witches in Apuleius imprison men for sexual use, routinely threaten them with castration, and enjoy urinating in their faces. It should also be borne in mind that the hero of this book is transformed into a donkey — an animal famous for its ample male organ. Our asinine protagonist is beaten through every adventure until, at last, he renounces sex forever at the behest of the powerful goddess Isis. The message is clear: all indulgence physical pleasure must be punished, the flesh is evil. The occasional lovely young witch we see in later literature is a refinement of the witch as emblem of body-hatred, not a remission of it.

A clear progression should now be apparent: Circe in Homer is a goddess and inspirer of passion. Medea is demoted to hero in Pindar and the dramatists, who make her the *victim* of passion. The witches of Apollonius and Theocritus are simply love-sick girls. The Roman witches who follow, where not deliberate imitations of earlier literary figures (e.g. Ovid's Medea), carry on the degenerative trend — the witches are now lust-crazed hags and living dead sex-cannibals.

Alongside the aging witch we find a paradoxical young and lovely one, but this is marginal to the overall trend, and the beautiful sorceresses are described as cruel and sadistic: they are merely a deceptively attractive variant on the same degenerating image.

The process is not a piece of malice on the part of the poets, and apparently unconscious. Its persistence for a thousand year period, *never before remarked*, calls for some explanation. The easiest one, misogyny, is contradicted by the far from gynophobic character of the writers cited, which is even more significant when we bear in mind the really great temporal and geographic range of our sources.

More importantly, it is only at the end of her development, when the witch has been demoted to merely human status, that we find assertions that witchcraft is something basic to womankind: were misogyny the source and not a final result of the witch mythology, we would expect some borrowing during its first 800 years from the real if marginal Greek tradition of misogynistic literature.

Nigra Sum Sed Formosa

I am black but comely. O daughters of Jerusalem
— Song of Solomon

The witches are masters of one single and sovereign science — the use of herbs. Herbs are the most important ingredient in all classical magic and indeed of classical (and modern) medicines.

There are some interesting confirmations of this from antiquity. An oblique one comes from the second-century AD Alexandrian scholar Dionysus Skytobrachion, who tried to explain away Hecate by making her a historical person. He described her as the founder of toxicology, and said that Circe and Medea were her her daughters! Though this is laughable as history, it is a valuable document of how the ancients viewed witches' work.

More direct and less exotic testimony comes from the first-century BC Roman encyclopaedist Pliny. In the twenty-fifth chapter of his *Natural History* he says explicitly that herbs are the primary tool used by witches. The relation of the witch (in Greek, *pharmakis*, literally "herbalist") to herbs is a thing so far unnoticed by scholars, and far more meaningful than might at first appear.

From the eighth century BC, when the poet Homer creates Circe with her "baleful herbs" (in Greek, *pharmaka lugra*), to the latest Roman conjure-women of the second century BC, the witches use, almost exclusively, and always primarily, plants. Circe's herbs turn Odysseus men into animals — and it is only by using a counter-herb, *moly*, that Odysseus can resist her charms.

In the Homeric *Hymn to Demeter*, the disguised goddess of agriculture promises to protect the child Demophon from the charms of herb-gatherers, that is, witches. In Euripides' play *Medea*, that heroic sorceress promises king Aegaeus herbal medicines that will end his childlessness.

The poet Apollonius' description of Medea defines herbalizing as the most awesome and impressive of witch activities:

... and Medea took from the wooden box
a medicine which men call Promethean.
If a man should anoint his body with it,
having first appeased Hecate with nocturnal sacrifice,
that man could not be wounded
by the stroke of bronze weapon, nor need he flinch
from blazing fire. For the length of a day
he's invulnerable to both.
The Promethean plant first shot up from the soil
when the eagle, feasting on bound Prometheus' liver
high on the craggy side of Mount Caucasus,
let the divine blood of the immortal victim drip.
Where the blood touched soil, a flower appeared,
a foot-high plant that looked like a two-stalked
crocus,
but in the earth the root looked exactly like raw cut
flesh.

The juice of the plant, dark as the sap of a mountain
oak,
Medea had squeezed into a seashell and kept to make
this spell.
This is how she gathered the magic plant:
first she bathed in seven ever-flowing streams,

then called seven times on Hecate,
fosterer of all that's young,
night wandering Hecate, queen of the dead.

Medea made this invocation in blackest night,
wearing black garments.
Then she went for the plant, and as she pulled it out
    of the ground
and hacked off the fleshlike root,
Prometheus, chained up on his rock,
felt it as though she had cut into his own skin.
He groaned and, in response, the whole earth shook
and a bellowing was heard from under the ground.

Herbs are thus assuredly the primary means of magic. Euripides' Medea uses magical herbs in the work of a midwife, and to kill. Like her, all the post-Homeric witches will use herbs exclusively to bring about love and fertility, or to cause death. (There are only two exceptions to this rule in the 1200 year record of classical witchcraft. One is Circe's use of herbs to transform men into animals, which will be explained below. The other is Apollonius' Medea, who makes an herbal invulnerability ointment for Jason.)

Apollonius' contemporary Theocritus, writing poems set in the "modern" world of Hellenistic Alexandra, shows that herbs are used by the witches on the one hand as simple poisons, and on the other as love charms or aphrodisiacs. Simaitha, Theocritus' amateur witch, mentions the master love-herb Horsemad (in Greek, *Hippomanes*):

Horsemad is an herb that grows in Arcadia,
every filly or fast-running mare that eats it
gallops over the hills looking for a stallion.

May it do the same to the man who spurns me,
may I see him run from the gym to my door
raving with desire.

(Readers interested in acquiring a little Horsemad for their own use will have difficulty. *Hippomanes* was variously described in antiquity as a plant, the genital secretions of a rutting mare, or a caul-like thing on the head of a newborn foal, which the mother must eat in order to develop maternal instincts.)

Beyond love charms, Simaitha also intends to use herbs to poison the man she wants if he won't succumb. Sex and death: these are the cardinal concerns of all herbal witch work.

Before we go on to the Latin evidence, it will be worth observing, purely as an aside, that while herbs are the prime tool of *all* classical witchcraft, the Latins place an additional emphasis on *incantations*. In the oldest collection of Roman laws, the *Laws of the Twelve Tablets*, which go back to the fifth century BC, it is forbidden to "sing harmful spells."

The first-century AD poet Horace gives us in his *Epodes* the first mention ever of a book of spells. Horace' contemporary Ovid gives the same primacy to words in all his witch descriptions: "What *can't* song do?" he wonders aloud in his Medea story. (The Greeks never gave much thought to verbal spells: *The Greek Magical Papyri* do not constitute an exception. They were written in Egypt and drew on the Egyptian tradition of magic. The every tomb wall and coffin plank in Egypt attests Egypt's veneration for the text.)

Turning now to herbs in the literature of the Roman period, we see the Latin word *venenum* (poison) in place of the Greek *pharmakon* (herb"). This represents the ultimate telescoping of the functions of herbal magic. All is expressed in a single word which means primarily "poison" but also "love-charm." Of a piece with this prejudicial term for herbs, is the fact that herbs are now gathered in graveyards In Horace' *Satire*, Priapus complains his scarecrow tactics are useless against witches who invade the paupers' graveyard to carry out their love spells:

> . . . there's no way I can put an end to this business
> or stop them from gathering bones and harmful herbs
> in the graveyard as soon as the wandering moon
> shows her lovely pale face . . .

The substances employed by the witch begin to become a list of very assorted loathsomes. In one of his *Epodes*, Horace describes the love spell of a witch named Canidia who

> . . . orders her fellow witches to throw on the fire
> wood from wild fig trees uprooted from tombs,
> timber of the mournful cypress,
> eggs and feathers of a night-roving screech-owl
> smeared with the blood of a hideous toad,
> herbs grown in Medea's hometown on the Black Sea,
> herbs from poison-exporting Spain,
> bones snatched from the jaws of a starving bitch
> — all these go into the magic flames.

Still, herbs retain their centrality. Further, for Horace, the aim of gathering these exotic noxiousities, closer in mood to Macbeth's moors than Circe's island, is always love-magic,

Ovid, who brings his giddy sense of excess to the trope, remains within the fertility-death framework of witches' work, and indeed more entirely than any of his predecessors, for his Medea is heating a cauldron that will bring about old king Pelias' *death and rebirth*. Here too seeds, flowers and roots figure prominently.

Lucan, a first-century AD Roman poet from the generation after Horace and Ovid, shows us the witch Erictho who, like Medea, brings about an equivocal rebirth: she temporarily restores a dead soldier to life. The most interesting thing about Lucan's witch is that, in a stunning anticipation of the crop-blighting hags of the middle ages, she is pointedly hostile to plants. Lucan says of Erictho:

> Her tread blights the seeds of the fertile cornfield,
> her breath makes poisonous the harmless air.

She walks like an anti-Aphrodite. According to Hesiod, flowers sprang up at every step the love goddess took, and warm, pleasant breezes always blew around her. Erictho is the negative of Aphrodite, and her inversion of the love goddess' imagery is something more than a coincidence. Indeed, it holds the key to understanding the archetype of the witch. But for the moment it must suffice to note that positive or negative, the relation of the witch to herbs is always central and entirely constant. The deeper meaning of the trope will begin to appear when we view the herbs in their larger context, that is to say, their landscape.

Witches favor groves and hilltops for their work with a very remarkable consistency. Thus the eighth-century BC Homeric description of Circe's home goes:

> Within the forest glades they found the house of Circe,
> built of polished stone in a place of wide outlook . . .

Similarly Ovid in the first century AD.:

> ... the herb-clad hills and palace of Circe,
> daughter of the sun,
> full of manifold beasts.

and his Medea has, if not a hill, at least a grove

> She took her way to an ancient altar of Hecate,
> hidden in the deep shades of a forest.

which is important enough to be cited in Jason's oath to her:

> He swore he would be true
> by the sacred rites of the threefold goddess,
> by whatever divinity might be in that grove ...

Seneca, a mid-first-century AD Roman philosopher, wrote a play that describes a Medea culling her herbs on all the major mountains from Spain to Persia. In his epic poem on the Roman civil war, Seneca's nephew Lucan assures us that, in his day, the witches of Thessaly still went to the heights a-herbing.

Back in the third century BC, the time of Theocritus, writers who described witches began to favor urban settings. From here on the cemetery tended to replace the grove— probably for reasons of practical accessibility (though Horace was careful to choose a cemetery on the Esquiline *hill*). However, some of the witches of later classical literature remain obliquely faithful to tradition of witching on hilltops by performing their rites on *rooftops*.

Waters are also a standard feature of witch topography. Circe's attendants in Homer are literally river nymphs:

> . . . four maidens were her serving-women in the house.
> Children were they of the springs and groves,
> and of the sacred rivers that flow forth to the sea. . .

Ovid's Medea also herbalizes on river banks but, like hills, this feature seems to fade with time, outside of archaizing epic-style poetry.

The final feature we need here consider is the witches' retinue of wild animals, of which the best example is Homer's

> . . . and round about it were mountain wolves and lions,
> whom Circe herself had bewitched;
> for she gave them evil drugs.
> Yet these beasts did not rush upon my men,
> but pranced about them fawningly,
> wagging their long tails.
> And as when hounds fawn around their master
> as he comes from a feast,
> for he ever brings them tid-bits to soothe their temper,
> so about them fawned the stout-clawed wolves and lions . . .

— a description which is of course the model for all succeeding Circes. In his magical novel, *The Golden Ass*, Apuleius describes the witch Pamphile, who can turn men into beasts. Indeed, the plot of the novel revolves around the fortunes of a hero who has been turned into a donkey by witchcraft. Wild animals also accompany Lucan's witches:

> Every creature that has power to kill
> and was born to do mischief,
> dreads the Thessalian witches
> and serves them as hired killers.

The fierce tiger and the angry lion, king of beasts,
lick their hands and fawn upon them . . .

It may be objected that I am doing no more than identifying certain literary motifs that are repeated in successive witch depictions — and have only shown that Circe is the template for all later witches. I can reply that only some of the motifs, and not the most likely ones, are reliably repeated over the centuries. Others, that have every apparent right to become standard, such as Circe's magic wand, appear only the one time in Homer. Is it more reasonable to expect that the witch would always have a wild beast, and a hill and a stream nearby? Yet this is so from Homer's Circe to Lucan's Erictho 900 years later. Further, the three features, hill, streams and beasts, all fit together as symbols typically associated with the archetype of the fertility goddess.

Many scholars have noted that Circe with her beasts strongly suggests the archetype of the *Potnia Theron*, the "Mistress of the Wild Animals." Artemis, in Homer's *Iliad*, is a good literary example of this. Visual examples may be seen in the illustrations to this book which show the earliest Hekate. The goddess, in her iconic representation, has an entourage of fierce animals.

The "Mother of the Mountains" seal from Knossos shows a "Mistress of the Wild Animals" standing on a hill. (See the reproduction above in the chapter *She Is a Tree of Life*.) Not only the animals in this image, but the hill itself is a standard part of the symbolism of the fertility goddess: Cybele, the "mountain mother" offers a well-known instance of the image.

Let us return to the river-nymphs that we saw as Circe's attendants in Homer, and the rivers Medea haunts in Ovid's account. These, like the symbolic hill, are a classic part of the fertility goddess' iconography. The Greeks believed every spring was inhabited by a nymph — that is, a *fertility spirit*. The fertility and rebirth symbolism of water is too well known from the Bible, from the Jacobs magical fertility trough to the "rebirth" of baptism, to need further comment here.

It appears that the witch of literature, with her sacred landscape of plants, streams, animals and hills, and her focus on love and fertility magic, and even her special relation to the world of ghosts, recapitulates, in considerable and constant detail, the archetype of the fertility goddess. Of course, the figure of the witch does so on the unconscious level, and her content may *seem* to be a mere literary motif.

The topography of the witch, that magical landscape of an eternal Spring, appears to fade in literature as urbanization increases with the approach of the first century AD. But, in fact, the hills, beasts, plants and waters survive their own disappearance! The moment they vanish from the narratives, they all re-emerge in the witches' lists of their powers *over* nature, which ordinarily culminate in "drawing down the moon," in Greek, *kathairesis*. Thus Apollonius' Medea is credited with control of plants, rivers, the entire landscape — with a startling skyward extension:

> The maiden Medea, nurtured in the palace of king Aeetes
> — the goddess Hecate taught her to handle magic herbs
> with exceeding skill. Every plant the soil feeds
> or rivers water, she knows. By the power of her herbs,
> she can nullify the never-tiring power of fire itself,
> she can stay the course of rivers as they rush roaring on,
> and check the stars in their circuit,
> pause the swift course of the moon.

The witch-powers, that once suggested an *identification* with the earth, have now been inverted into an assault upon it. Ovid gives an even more exuberantly detailed account:

> O Night, faithful preserver of mysteries,
> and you, bright stars whose golden beams,
> together with the moon, follow the heat of day;
> you, three-formed Hecate, who know our undertakings
> and come to the aid of the spells and arts of magicians
> with your potent herbs;
> you breezes and winds,
> you mountains and streams and pools,
> all you gods of the groves, all you gods of the night
> — be with me now. With your help, when I have willed it,
> the streams have run back to their fountain-heads,
> while the banks wondered:
> I lay the swollen, and stir up calm seas by my spells;
> I drive the clouds and bring on the clouds;
> the winds I dispel and summon;
> I break the jaws of serpents with my incantations;
> living rocks and oaks I root from their own soil;
> I move the forests, I bid the mountains shake,
> the earth to rumble,
> and the ghosts to come forth from their tombs.
> Thee also, Moon, do I draw from the sky . . .
> even the chariot of the Sun, my grandsire,
> blanches at my song; the Dawn pales at my poisons

Here the entire landscape of the goddess is meticulously reproduced. (And so splendidly that Shakespeare borrowed it, with few changes, for Prospero's farewell to magic in *The Tempest*.)

It is interesting to note that, as the witch becomes more mortal (from Circe, who is a goddess in Homer, to the Roman crones), the witches' powers become more godlike. By late first century AD, in Latin poetry, the image of the drawing down of the moon proclaims an outright superiority to the gods — the spiritual equivalent of a military *coup*.

I hope the reader will forgive another digression to examine in detail the extremely appealing subject of "drawing down the moon." There is nothing in Greek or Roman mythology that could have provided a precedent for the witches' feat of pulling the moon out of the sky. The ancients themselves, who were not at all averse to rational explanations, sometimes interpreted "drawing down the moon" as a primitive way of accounting for lunar eclipse.

A far more intriguing idea is that the witches draw down the moon *in order to milk it*. The background to this is the notion (commonly held in Roman antiquity) that the moon drinks in mist which it later lets fall to the earth as dew. There are descriptions of moon-milking in Apuleius' novel and in Lucan's epic poem. In the latter, Erictho uses the lunar fluid to reanimate a corpse. Though Lucan doesn't explain the mechanics involved, I would guess that the operant concept is the moon's ability to be reborn from black nothingness.

In A. M. Tupet's useful book, *Magie dans la Poésie Latine*, there is an interesting account of modern-day North African folk-magic. There witches trap the moon by catching its reflection in a basin of water. The water appears to boil as the moon follows its image into the basin— for the moon is very cold. Once the water has absorbed the moon, it becomes a liquid useful in love spells.

The antiquity of the practice seems confirmed by an ancient commentary on *The Clouds*, a play by the fifth-century BC Greek Aristophanes. The commentator says that if you catch the reflection of the moon in a mirror and write on this with blood, the letters you inscribe on the polished surface should appear on the real moon as well. The commentator does not tell us the point of this sky-writing; perhaps no more is intended than a frightening display of magic power.

A "drawing down the moon" more precisely parallel to the one Tupet cites is given in a spell in the *Greek Magical Papyri*. Here the moon is fixed by the magician's special knowledge of her attributes, such as only an initiate into her religious mysteries would possess. These attributes make up an extensive list of adjectives, alternative names and mystic emblems of the deity — *e.g.*, sandal, key, wheel. The moon is then trapped in her reflection. The magician says:

> Look at yourself in this bowl of Nile water
> that serves as a mirror,
> and as you see yourself you're amazed —
> blinded by your own light
> — before you see clear again
> you'll do what I force you to do . . .

More secret attributes are then are given, and very strange they are, ranging from "an old sieve" to "the well-penetrated vagina of a black sphinx." The magician then threatens to disorder the entire cosmos (hide the sun at noon, send the ocean onto land, &c.) unless the moon goddess rage against the magician's intended victim.

Once "drawing down the moon" appears as a standard witchly accomplishment, which it does in the first century AD, the witches' powers begin to extend, like Hecate's, over all three worlds, flickering the stars, bursting open the earth, reversing the rivers and tempesting the sea. The witches will, if we may use an audacious metaphor, *shake the world-tree* and make tremble all the realms. As the philosopher-playwright Seneca's Medea threatens: "I shall shake all that is!" And indeed this Medea attacks the gods and pulls down the sky. Lucan gives the witches powers no less cosmic:

Because of the witches, natural changes cease to operate:
daylight lingers and is delayed by the length of night;
outer space is disobedient to the laws of physics.
Listening to their spells, the planets stop in mid-orbit,
and Zeus, who keeps the cosmos spinning as it should,
is amazed at the sudden standstill.
At one time the witches may drench the world with rain,
veil the hot sun with clouds,
and make the heavens thunder without Zeus' permission;
also, by their spells, they disperse the sky's canopy of watery
    vapor
and tear away the disheveled tresses of the storm clouds.

Or else, though the winds are still, the witches make the seas rise
    high;
or again they may forbid the ocean to be affected by storms,
and keep it silent while the South wind blusters,
and the sails that speed a vessel belly out with the breeze.
The witches can arrest water falls halfway down
a steep cliff-face, they make the running rivers forsake
their downward channels and flow backwards upstream.
They make the Nile fail to rise in summer,
they make the Meander straighten its course,
they make slow rivers speed and rapid ones go stagnant-still;

they flatten landscapes, the mountains
lower their tops and level their ridges
so Mount Olympus looks up at the clouds above it.
They make Siberian snows thaw
without any sun, in winter's cold.
When the tide is driven in by the moon,
the spells of witches drive it back and keep the shore dry.

They destabilize the earth, make it wobble on its axis,
so it's night at noonday, and up in the sky

182

you see all the wrong constellations. . .

The stakes have now been raised to the point where it is fair to call the witch a goddess once again. One should note here that the original goddess topography — the hills and rivers and vegetation — are meticulously preserved in all the accounts.

At this point I may profitably examine in somewhat more detail the two witch preoccupations, fertility and death, which I noted above in our consideration of herbs. It is these that define the witch as actively a descendant of the Earth Mother, who is both womb and tomb to all who come to life. As may be anticipated, the positive traits survive inverted. I mentioned Euripides' play in which Medea promises King Aegeus drugs to overcome his childlessness. This is the only instance of the witch's normal relation to the theme. Horace' witches typically steal children. Apuleius' Meroe closes the womb of a sexual rival so her pregnancy continues indefinitely, swelling her to elephantine size. Birth-magic is only part of the fertility paradigm: virtually all the witches' spells are directed to compelling sexual desire.

Let us now examine of the other side of the archetype — the witches' special relation to death. Already the sites of life, hilltops and springs, have been superseded by those that suggest the nearness of death, what one might call the "stations of the crossroads." Cemeteries and the midnight hour are preferred for rites that are almost always modeled on the necromancy Odysseus performs in the *Odyssey* — and that was performed, be it recalled, according to Circe's instructions.

The Homeric necromancy differs from its successors in one important detail — Homer's dead are weak things, fluttery shades that feebly squeak, like insubstantial bats.

These are angular shadows that fly crying through the infinite underworld night. They survive in the least material aspects of their mortal being, shadow and echo. Nothing transcendent about these creatures, and no new awareness. They are exactly what they were in life, only less so. Homer speaks of them as "not having the strength to hold up their own heads" — numbed nodding creatures on the verge of tottering back into absolute non-being. Even Tiresias receives no new or special qualities — he can advise of the future because he's Tiresias, not because he's passed the limits of mortality.

How different are the dead to whom the witches appeal! Needy and dangerous figures waiting in the shadows of existence. And the witches choose the ghosts they will control with an evil refinement — they particularly want the spirits of those who died young or violently, the unhappy and unsatisfied dead with their restless energy and free-floating rage. Thus children are the ideal subjects for necromancy. Consider the powers of the angry prepubescent dead, depicted in the speech of a boy Horace' witches are starving to death:

> Your magic spells have no the power to alter right and wrong,
> nor to avert human justice. The curse I utter now will hound
> you,
> no sacrifice will ever placate me or turn aside my grudge.
> No, when I, whom you have doomed, will have breathed my
> last,
> I'll return by night as a vengeful spirit, and as a ghost I'll come
> and tear
> at your faces with my crooked claws: such is the power of the
> dead!
> I'll seat myself on your racing hearts and terror of me will keep
> you from sleep.

An even more interesting, because non-literary, document of the how the angry dead were viewed is found in this spell from the *Greek Magical Papyri*:

Come, Hecate, goddess
of the crossroads, who with your fire-breathing phantoms
have dominion over scary roads
and harsh enchantments.
Hecate I call you,
and with you those untimely passed
away, the strong dead, those who died
before they could have a wife and children,
hissing wildly, yearning in their hearts.

Though the dead are ordinarily employed as agents in the witches' most characteristic activity — sending love spells or terrorizing those who do not erotically submit — the dead have their own associations and powers that effectively complete our picture of the witch.

There is a universal belief that the dead can see the future, that they *know everything*. For them time does not exist as it does for us who measure it by successive days. They inhabit the earth's black dream, the womb of every day, the belly of fate from which all that occurs arises briefly to our sight — they have passed decisively beyond the limits of the human condition, including that partial knowledge confined to what light reveals. Accordingly, in Lucan's epic the arch-witch Erictho asks about future from a common soldier whose only qualification is being dead.

Setting aside the matter of the dead imparting to witches their more than mortal knowledge, the mere fact that the dead can *return at all*, though only to be questioned, is a violent reversal of the ordinary laws and course of time. Thus there is a logic to the re-emergence of Chaos in necromantic rites. We see this where Ovid's Circe is threatened by Picus' followers:

> But she sprinkled upon them her baleful drugs
> and poisonous juices, summoning to her aid
> Night, and the gods of Night, from Erebus,
> and Chaos, calling on Hecate
> in long-drawn, wailing cries.
> The woods, wonderful to say,
> leaped from their place, the ground rumbled,
> the neighboring trees turned white,
> and the herbage where her poisons fell
> was stained with clots of blood.
> The stones also seemed to voice hoarse bellowings;
> the baying of dogs was heard, the ground
> was foul with dark, crawling things,
> and the insubstantial shades of the dead
> seemed to be flitting about.

Chaos appears again in *The Golden Ass*, where the witch Pamphile

> . . . is considered the most consummate magician and necromancer. By breathing out words and charms over plants and minerals and other seemingly trivial things, she can throw the stars down into the bottom of hell, and return them to the condition of primordial chaos.

Lucan's Erictho is on a first-name basis with Chaos. She says,

> I invoke the Furies, the horror of Hell,
> the punishments of the guilty, and Chaos,
> eager to blend countless worlds into one indistinct ruin. . .

So does Seneca's Medea, and Dido, the lover of the hero Aeneas in Virgil's first-century AD epic. Dido is an accomplished witch. Vergil says:

186

   . . . Dido, dark priestess, calls in thunder tones
   on thrice a hundred gods,
   Erebus and Chaos, and threefold Hecate . . .

Hecate herself is finally identified with Chaos in the *Magical Papyri*, where she is invoked with phrases like "Primal Chaos," "Chaos, too, you rule" and simply addressed as "broad Chaos."

I feel that the figure of the witch herself may best be understood as a survival of the archetype of the fertility goddess. Her original divinity was demonstrated in the previous chapter. I have reviewed in this one her recapitulation of the fertility goddess' iconography. The witch's ghosts and her invocations of Chaos are also a part of the symbolism of the fertility goddess, particularly as it appears in the context of *new year's rites*.

The principles at play in these festivals of agricultural societies is that the inauguration of the new year repeats the cosmogonic act, the creation, which requires first a return to the state of chaos whence order arose. This is symbolized in a number of ways (carnival license, &c.) but primarily through the return of the dead whom the abrogation of all limits (including those of time) has now brought back into contact with the living. Mircea Eliade's copious documentation of the new year pattern cannot be here presented in full — one apt example must suffice: In European tradition, during the twelve intercalary days preceding the new year in mid-winter, the dead come in procession to visit their families, led by one of the chthonic-funerary fertility goddesses (Holda, Perchta, &c.). The analogy of Hecate and the spook-horde with the European version is clear, and the near eastern antiquity of the motif is evident from the Sumerian poem *Inanna's Descent to the Nether World*. Describing Inanna's return from her unsuccessful attempt to extend the rule of life over the world of the dead, the poem says:

> When Inanna returns from the nether world,
> truly, the dead hasten ahead of her . . .

To Hecate, Holda and Inanna we may now add a degenerated heir of the symbolism, the rotting goddess who is the Graeco-Roman witch. This is supported by her special relation to a liminal region of time, though the uncorrupted deity leads her ghost-horde at the turning of the year and the witch bullies her few straggling spooks across the midpoint of a single night. There is more. The carnival amorality of the New Year celebration has its parallel in the witches' transcendence of sexual norms and limits, as their love-magic bears witness.

Looking over the assembled traits of the final Roman witch figure, and asking ourselves what she means, in an existential sense, in the context of late antiquity's civilized discontent, religious dissatisfaction, and desperate desire to refresh an existence sick with history by a renewal of time itself, we may begin to appreciate the inverted grandeur and ambivalent, millennial fascination of the witch, who is, on this level, a one-woman apocalypse, a terrifying female avatar of chaos, a violent outbreak of the forces of the Beginning in a world that felt itself nearing the End.

The Witch of Endor

Despite its large authority in European law and legend, the Biblical account of witchcraft is all too brief. But a few interesting and as yet undiscovered details can be wrung from this material, particularly when we juxtapose it with the classical sources. All the detailed mentions of witchcraft in the Bible seem to equate it with the practice of Canaanite religion. One passage, the earliest mention of witchcraft in the Bible, may here be cited in full. Micah (late eighth century BC) writes:

> In that day
>> — declares the Lord —
> I will destroy the horses in your midst
> And wreck your chariots.
> I will destroy the cities of your land
> And destroy all your fortresses.
> I will destroy all your sorcerers,
> And you shall have no more spell-crooners.
> I will destroy your idols
> And the phallic stones for Baal in your midst;
> And no more shall you bow down
> To the work of your hands.
> I will tear down the sacred poles of Ashtoreth in your midst
> And destroy your idols.

In the Biblical condemnations, the worship of Ashtoreth is always mentioned alongside witchcraft as an "abominable practice," thus we may expect that the Canaanite goddess stood in some relation to the Witch of Endor comparable to that of Hecate to, for example, Medea.

We meet the witch of Endor in *The First Book of Samuel* in the Bible. The story is set in the eleventh century BC. King Saul, a monotheist, has outlawed witchcraft. Now, at the low-ebb of his fortunes, he calls on the witch who lives near the town of Endor, to have her summon the soul of the dead prophet Samuel. Samuel is to be asked whether Saul and his sons will survive their battle with the Philistines the next day. Saul visits the witch at night, and in disguise: it is a furtive, illegal consultation.

The witch performs her divining in an *ecstatic* state.. At first she does not recognize the disguised Saul — *only when she has gone into her trance* (for she, not Saul, sees the ghost of Samuel), is she able to *see through* Saul's disguise. Evidently she has transcended the limits of human knowledge and power, she has gone into ecstasy. To what extent is ecstasy common to all witchcraft?

Although we have no account of Ashtoreth being a sender of trance or madness in the extremely sparse textual record, we have abundant documentation for other and cognate goddesses from the region, such as Cybele and especially Hecate, who are *ordinarily* given this description. The classical witches *always* go into frenzy for their rites. For example, the Roman stoic philosopher Seneca wrote a play about Medea, in which a character says of her: "I've often seen her raving, staggering, stunned." Too much should not be made of the ecstasy as a mark of neolithic religiosity — ecstasy is basic to *all* levels of religious culture, from the hunter-gatherer shamans, through the bacchantes of a world in awe of the mysteries of agriculture, to the solitary mystics of scriptural religion. Still, common as ecstasy is to every period, it is far from common to *everyone* in a given period, and so it constitutes an important link between the two worlds of witchery.

As the world of the dead, the world underground, is a central and legitimate concern of the fertility goddess, so it is for the women associated with her. It is the best-attested object of classical witchcraft, from Homer's Circe, who advises Odysseus on how to raise the ghost of the prophet Tireias and cause him to utter the future, to the Roman poet Lucan's witch Erictho, who raises the ghost of a republican soldier to foretell the results of the battle between Caesar and Pompey at Pharsalus. In this connection, the interrogation of the dead, we find the most valuable link between the witches of Greece and Israel: a sound which emerges from the *ov* or "ghost-bottle."

The most common epithet applied to the witch of Endor, and all the other Hebrew witches, is *baalat ov*, "possessor of an *ov*." In ordinary use, the Hebrew word *ov* means a skin used to hold water or wine. Unfortunately, the biblical account doesn't actually describe the witch using her *ov*. To figure out what it was, we have to gather clues from several places.

Parallels to the notion of ghosts or spirits residing in a bottle or gourd are many, from the lamp-inhabiting genies of the *Arabian Nights* to the bottle-gourd of China, itself a symbol of necromancy and attribute of the Taoist Immortal Li Tieh-Kui, who is typically represented holding a bottle gourd from which spirals of smoke ascend, indicating his ability to leave his body at will in spirit form. Fans of Hong Kong horror films are well familiar with the ceramic jars in which Taoist sorcerers keep the ghosts they force to serve them.

But we can clarify the *ov* from sources closer to hand. Our knowlege of Canaanite religion is based on Israeli archaeology, references in the Bible and, most importantly, the texts of Ugarit. This last is a thirteenth-century BC library unearthed in the early twentieth century in a lost city on the coast of Syria. It gives detailed mythological accounts of the gods worshiped in Canaan, in a language that scholars call Ugaritic, which is nearly identical to Biblical Hebrew. And, in fact, shared images and whole borrowed lines make it clear that the epic poetry of ancient Canaan was known and used by the poetical writers of the Bible as much as classical mythology was by Milton in *Paradise Lost*.

The Ugaritic texts contain the word *ilib*, which seems to mean "ancestral spirit," and we should probably take this to mean "spirit of the bottle." The word *il* means god or otherworld being, and is cognate with the Hebrew word *el* ("god"). The world *ib*, meaning bottle, is cognate with the Hebrew word *ov*. (Fuller and fascinating detail about this etymology is found in Theodor Gaster's *Myth, Legend and Custom in the Old Testament*, where he offers many interesting insights into the Witch of Endor story.)

Another piece of evidence that helps us see that the "ghost-bottle" or *ov* of the Witch of Endor was intended to hold a spirit comes from the Septuagint's rendering of the word *ov*. The Septuagint is a translation of the Hebrew Bible into Greek, made at Alexandria in the third to first centuries BC. Scholars value the Septuagint because the translators may have had better copies of the biblical texts, or a better understanding of them, than we now possess. After all, ancient Israel still existed then, so there were living authorities to consult.

The Septuagint always translates the word *ov* with the Greek word *engastrimuthos*, meaning literally "belly-speaker." This was a person who delivered oracles in a strangely altered voice, perhaps using ventriloquism. An ethnographic parallel that helps draw together all the evidence, is provided by the *govi* or ancestral spirit jar of

Haitian Voodoo. A year after a family member's death, the soul of the deceased is summoned, with the aid of the voodoo priest, to reside in the *govi* jar on the altar. Here it can be venerated and, through the priest, it may be consulted on behalf of the living. We have an eyewitness account from Maya Deren in her book *Divine Horsemen*, which describes the sound the priest causes to proceed from the *govi*:

> . . . the summoned voice in the govi . . . is an objective oracular authority that booms as if from the bowels of the earth.

Another important characteristic of the *ov* is the special kind of sound that emerges from it. The most frequently used epithets of the Hebrew witch all relate to *sounds*. She is a "crooner," *m'onen* (from *anan*, a word whose Arabic cognate seems to mean "to hum"); she is a "hisser," *m'nahesh*, a term related to the word *nahash*, "serpent." The eighth-century BC prophet Isaiah describes witches as making special spooky sounds:

> Now, should people say to you, "Inquire of those who have a ghost-bottle and the diviners that chirp and coo; for a people may inquire of the spirit world, of the dead on behalf of the living. . ."

and

> Your speech shall sound like a ghost-bottle (*ov*), it shall come from underground,
> Your voice shall chirp from the region where you are buried.

Now the Graeco-Roman dead speak in similar funereal chirps to Homer's Odysseus, when he performs his

193

necromancy. Seven hundred years later the Latin poet Horace depicts witches who extort sounds "sad and shrill" from the dead in a cemetery on the Esquiline hill in Rome.

Rather than fatiguing the reader with the copious Graeco-Roman record of necromantic bird-calls, I will offer a cross cultural comparison. This comes from the Norse witches, priestesses of Freya, the Great Goddess and fertility figure of the North, who mediumistically speak for the dead in magic chants called *galdr*, from the verb *galan*, "to sing" — a word used especially with reference to bird song.

The logic behind the chirpings of the ghost-bottle, and the classical and Nordic spooks is a symbolic one: the dead are imagined with the voices of birds as an emblem of their transcendence of the limits of the body: they are free and can "fly". The same concept is behind the *ba* or soul-bird of Egypt and the winged angels of Christian Europe.

Into the Cauldron

The Graeco-Roman witch, due to her ecstatic rites and mysterious access to the world of ghosts and spirits, was a natural magnet for folkloric material relating to shamanism. This was a late but fascinating addition to the mythology of the witch. There have been a few attempts by scholars to show a connection between far northern and Siberian shamanism and various shadowy ancient figures of Greek myth like the Thracian prophet Zalmoxis, and Abaris, the sage of the mythical land Hyperborea. The mysterious religion of the Orphics has also been pondered for its shamanic content. Even features of early philosophy, such as the magical flight described in Parmenides' great poem, have excited interest for possible traces of shamanism.

A vestige of shamanism may perhaps be seen in the *goes* (pronounced "go ace,") a Greek word meaning "howler"). The term *goes* was generally applied to professional practitioners in the Orphic-magical-Dionysiac mystery tradition, to mountebanks and charlatans, healers and fortune-tellers, in fine, to every sort of paid purveyor of supernatural thrills. In addition, though less usually, the word could be used to refer to shape-shifters, like the Scythian werewolves mentioned by Herodotus.

The word *goes* does have a shamanic ring to it. One of the shaman's standard functions is to lead dead souls to their place of rest in the underworld. He does this through an ecstatic performance, in the course of which he "becomes" various gods and animal spirits, that is, he impersonates for his audience, vocally and in mime, many of the figures in his supernatural journey. The *goes* of classical Greece, with his dealings with the dead, spiritual pretensions, and name that suggests animal howls and shape-shifting, may be a late debased survival of the shaman.

But I don't need to pronounce on the shamanic motifs in Greek literature here, because none of these are ever related to the *witches*. Even the best attested of the Greek shamanic motifs, the rather general term *goes*, is never applied to a witch, though the term seems appropriate to individuals who ordinarily go into ecstatic states for their rites and have an ongoing traffic with the spirit world.

The Greek shamanic lore that remained from ancient Indo-European sources and what arrived in accounts that came south from Scythia (Russia), constituted too feeble a trickle of influence to make the shamanic a powerful current in Greek supernatural thinking. The Greeks typically turned their political ambitions east, south and west, and took little notice of the fur-clad barbarians up north. The Romans, on the other hand, were peculiarly concerned with the primitively equipped races they could so handily defeat. These barbarians, in direct contact with their Roman foes, are the most plausible source for the shamanic lore which (as I shall strive to show) enriched the Roman witch depiction.

Simply defined, a shaman is an individual in an archaic society who is able to enter ecstatic states or trances in which he travels through other worlds — heavens and underworlds — typically on healing missions, such as to cure a sick man by finding his strayed or stolen soul. The shaman first achieves this ability in a spiritual crisis which it would be fair to call a death, since it places him decisively outside the limits of the human condition. During this "death" he characteristically suffers dismemberment and the replacement of his organs with immortal equivalents, makes an ascent through the heavens and a descent through the underworld. All this takes place on the spiritual plane, of course, while his body remains comatose. In the course of his terrific journey the shaman acquires spiritual helpers, the ability to take on the shapes of animals, to speak in the tongues of all creatures and even of the gods, and achieves mastery of fire (handling coals, &c.).

We shall follow this mystical itinerary in our survey of the classical literature, giving in each case examples from the witchcraft of the Roman period and parallels from Eliade's study, *Shamanism, Archaic Techniques of Ecstasy*, which remains the classic exposition of the subject.

1: Crisis — Death State

The shaman's first initiatory seizure, and to some extent all his succeeding trances, are "deaths" — excursions beyond the limits of the human condition and the borders of mortality. He can see the souls of the dead and share in their uncanny knowledge because he too has experienced death and is, though alive, also "dead." He signalizes this by modes of behavior appropriate to the dead, such as comatose states. He also dresses in a post-mortem style: the Siberian shaman's costume is typically ornamented with iron objects that represent bones — he wears his skeleton on the outside, visible like that of a man long dead.

In the same spirit, the Roman witches operate at the hour when ghosts are abroad — "the silent center of the night" in the words of the first-century BC Roman poet Tibullus. And it is only in Roman literature that the graveyard became the site for witching, and that corpse became a primary magical tool. Lucan's Erictho is the most fully realized portrayal of this living-dead witch:

To her it was a crime to shelter her accursed head in a city or under a roof. Dear to the deities of Hell, she inhabited deserted tombs and haunted graves from which the ghosts had been driven. Neither the gods of Heaven, nor the fact that she was still living, prevented her from hearing the speechless conversation of the dead, or from knowing the abodes of Hell and the mysteries of subterranean Pluto. Haggard and loathsome with age is the face of the witch; her awful countenance is overcast with a hellish pallor and weighed down by uncombed locks, it is never seen by sunlight . . .

This extreme image is characteristic of the Roman witches and entirely at odds with the lovely witches of Greece: Circe, Medea, Simaitha! The funerary is a new element, and one that will endure. We may perhaps see in the witches' acquisition of shamanic death-garb the origin of the black-robed graveyard glamour we associate with the witch today.

2: Dismemberment

Once in the deathlike state that is part of the spiritual crisis of initiation, the shaman is — on the spiritual plane — hewn apart, often boiled in a cauldron, then rebuilt with immortal equivalents of his former organs. A similar event is associated with the later witches. Apuleius tells us how the witch Meroe put her runaway love-slave into a deep magical sleep during which she slit open his throat, reached down into his entrails, and pulled out his heart! This loss to his circulatory system she made good by inserting a charmed sponge. He lived, and was in fact unaware of the loss he had sustained. Elsewhere in the novel, the hapless Thelyphron was similarly hexed into a "deathlike" sleep, he was "dead asleep" and "buried in slumber." The witches then cut off his nose and ears, replacing them with wax copies. A close parallel is provided by the initiation of the Araucian shaman of South America, cited by Eliade, whose nose or eyes may be torn off and exchanged with those of his initiator.

The Roman poet Ovid says that, among the carefully chosen substances of Medea's rejuvenation brew that will *replace* the blood of old Aeson, are stones — "pebbles sought in the farthest Orient. . . " Likewise Lucan's Erictho replaces the innards of the corpse she will return to unhappy and equivocal life with stones ". . . that rattle when warmed under a breeding eagle. . . "

Stones are popular as organ-replacements in shamanic initiation world wide, as among the Wotjobalak tribesmen of Australia, where rock-crystals are especially favored.

The logic of the stones lies in rock's immediate implication of superhuman immutability and duration, of immortality, which would explain why this substance is the most universal choice for funerary monuments.

Boiling the dismembered body *in a cauldron* is also recorded: this, says Ovid, is Medea's procedure when she rejuvenates an old ram (to show that her magic will really work) and again when she pretends to do the same for the aged Pelias.

The poet Propertius, Ovid's near contemporary, shows us a witch who also possesses a cauldron. To be sure, one brass pot does not a shamaness make, but when we note that she is also a shape-shifter, able ". . . to disguise her shape with the form of the night-prowling wolf. . . ", we are entitled to see in the cauldron part of the shamanic pattern.

That the witch is the agent and not the subject of the dismemberment procedure does not compromise the idea of shamanic influence. Such distortion is to be expected when a religious reality travels far to become folklore. What is of

moment is the constant constellation of ideas —
dismemberment, organ-replacement, death-state, cauldron
— over and over again, in the larger framework of shamanic
motifs I will set forth in the course of this essay.

It should be noted that this is the first era in which the
witch appears *with cauldron*, a feature whose later
prominence needs no comment.

3: Ascent

After the physical renovation that finalizes his post-mortem
and more-than-mortal state, the shaman characteristically
makes an ascent to heaven to meet the gods and receive from
them the secrets of shamanizing. Typically he does so on the
back of, or in the form of, a bird. For this reason birdly
features, from decorative feathers to full-body bird disguise,
are typical of the shaman's costume.

The witches also turn into birds: Ovid ponders whether
screech owls aren't witches who have shifted shape, while
Apuleius gives this detailed account:

> . . . first I saw how Pamphile put off all her garments, and took
> out wooden boxes. She opened one and warmed the ointment
> therein with her fingers, and then rubbed her body with it from
> the sole of the foot to the crown of the head. When she had
> whispered much over the lamp, she shook her whole body, and
> as her arms gently moved I perceived how plumes grew out on
> them, and how they grew into strong wings. Her nose became
> crooked and hard, her nails turned into claws, and Pamphile
> became an owl. She cried and screeched to try her powers,
> fluttered up from the ground by little and little, till at last she
> leaped up and flew quite away.

Here we see another motif familiar from European witch lore, the "flying ointment" the witches use to travel to the Sabbath, on the backs of their familiar spirits or else in animal form themselves.

4: Descent

There is only one classical example of this shamanic motif, but it is so rich and complex as to make it a standard and touchstone for all others. Unfortunately, its great length prohibits quotation here. In view of this amazing text it will be clear that neither the necromancy in Homer's Odyssey nor any of the pre-Roman witch-rites are particularly *shamanic*, whatever their funereal overtones. Though a shaman can see ghosts, not everyone who sees a ghost is a shaman.

The account in question is Book Six of Lucan's *Civil War*. There the witch Erictho makes an explicit descent to the world of the dead through a mountain cave *to summon back from Hades a newly dead soul and force it to re-enter its own corpse*. Shamans ordinarily make such descents to the world of the dead in order to hale hence the strayed or stolen soul of an ill person.

5: Animal Transformation

Shamans, many of whose helper spirits are animals, access their power by taking on their forms (i.e., imitating their sounds and movements). Now the witches can change, not only into birds, but into virtually any animal. Apuleius tells us:

... witches change their skins and turn themselves at will into all kinds of beasts, and their disguises would deceive the eyes even of the all-seeing sun, or the eyes of Justice itself. Sometimes they change into birds, sometimes into dogs and mice, and sometimes into flies ...

A more direct echo of the shamanic motif is the witches' use of animal-sound in their incantations. This is the description of Erictho's the magic chant from Lucan's epic:

... and lastly her voice, more powerful than any magic herbs to rule over the powers of Hell, first uttered indistinct sounds, tuneless melodies, far different from human speech. The dog's bark and the wolf's howl were in that voice; it resembled the complaint of the restless owl and the night-flying screech-owl, the shrieking and roaring of wild beasts, the serpent's hiss, the beat of waves dashing against rocks, the sound of forests, and the thunder that issues from a rift in the cloud: in that one voice all these things were heard.

Here we have gone beyond animal transformation and touched on the shaman's power to make use of the language of spirits, in St. Paul's phrase, to "speak in the tongues of men and angels."

6: Language of the Gods

The shaman learns, in the course of his initiatory journey, the "language of the gods," which contains every sound and cry in the natural world, and is a sort of auditory microcosm.

This concept is developed explicitly in an invocation to the moon from *The Greek Magical Papyri*. The moon, whose cycles are described as the pattern of all being, is associated with a cosmic range of sounds. In the spell, the magician describes the sounds. (Magically, that is the same as actually producing them.)

> And the first companion of your name is silence, the second a popping sound, the third groaning, the fourth hissing, the fifth a cry of joy, the sixth moaning, the seventh barking, the eighth bellowing, the ninth neighing, the tenth a musical sound, the eleventh a sounding wind, the twelfth a wind-creating sound, the thirteenth a coercive sound, the fourteenth a coercive emanation of perfection.

The grandiose abstraction of some of these sounds suggests something more than mortal: the (to humans) unintelligible language of spirits. From the magician's *hocus pocus* to the archaic language of traditional liturgy to charismatic "speaking in tongues, the use of gibberish to symbolize the language of spirits is universal. The metaphysical cacophony of the passage above is an clear instance of the archetype.

7: Mastery of Fire

As a demonstration of his transcendent condition, the shaman can handle fire or walk on coals. It is a proof of this order that Erictho provides:

> . . . but if storm and black clouds take away the stars, then she issues forth from rifled tombs and tries to catch the nocturnal lightnings.

The Buryat of Siberia give a shaman's burial to anyone struck by lightning and consider his close relatives entitled to become shamans. The Soyot and Kamchdal believe that lightning flashes (without impact) can signify someone's shamanic election. There is also record of an Eskimo shaman who obtained his power after being struck by a "ball of fire."

Two insights emerge from our review of shamanic motifs in witch-depiction. First, meaningful echoes of shamanism only appear in witch mythology as of the first century BC. Ecstasy and necromancy, witch characteristics from the start, favored the assimilation of shamanic lore, but are themselves neutral. The late enrichment of the witch myth with shamanism is probably to be attributed simply to the Romans' large military involvement in, and thus contact with, the barbarian world where shamanism was practiced.

Second, we have identified the deeper meaning of a number of well-known features of the witchcraft known to European literature and art — funereal garb, flying ointment and animal transformation. These motifs were introduced into the mythology of the witch via the brilliant poetic creations of Ovid, Lucan and Apuleius.

Conclusion

I have shown, through all of Hecate's adaptations and evolutions, a steady demonization of her originally benign traits. The full outline of the figure so prejudicially treated only came into view as we turned our attention from Hecate to her followers, the witches. They effectively displaced and fully represented her by the end of antiquity.

I have noted that the witches finally attain godlike powers, and this trend is paralleled by the steady waning of Hecate. In fact, so peripheral does Hecate rapidly become that the only passages in which she actually *appears* are in book three of the Apollonius of Rhodes' third-century BC epic, *The Argonautica*, and in the satirist Lucian's second-century AD comic sketch *The Lover of Lies*. Even these two sources don't include enough description to make a full sentence. There exists nothing comparable to even these paltry depictions in the earlier (Greek) or later (mainly Latin) literature.

And these appearances are just that — appearances. Nowhere in the extant classical literature does Hecate speak even a word. In the face of Hecate's silence there was no recourse but to put our questions to the witches.

These proved to be, in all their constant details, a faithful reflection of the fertility goddess, of which archetype Hecate is a parade example. I was brought to the novel conclusion that the actual practice of witchcraft — that is, private magical activity centered on Hecate as a source of power and not just any casual practice of magic, herbalizing or midwifery — is perhaps the result and not the basis of the witch, who is at first a *mythological* figure.

The first account of Greek witchcraft as something contemporary and real is in the second *Idyll* of Theocritus, written in the third century BC, approximately 400 years after Hesiod formalized Hecate's entrance into the Greek pantheon. Chronologically, the sequence is half a millennium of Hecate-vilification and heroic-literary witches (like Medea) before actual contemporary witchcraft appears.

Carlo Ginzburg's book, *Night Battles* has shown how the same classical witch literature, in the hands of inquisitors, produced not only innocent victims but, as propaganda, finally persuaded many simple practitioners of agricultural magic that they were indeed "witches," and finally made some so in fact. The same myth had the same effect more than a thousand years before. The witches in Theocritus and later follow a *literary* not a ritual tradition.

The conclusion is reinforced by the fact that there was never an original basis in Hecate worship for witchcraft. But if the witch is just the goddess reduced to a folklore motif, and the real witches are a tardy result of that folklore, we must now repeat the question we have already and often posed — why was the fertility goddess so resolutely demonized?

The best explanation would be that here we have another instance of that same Greek dualism which Rhode, Nilsson, Picard and Guthrie — a century of classical scholarship — has described, I feel correctly, in terms of a conflict between indigenous Mediterranean and Indo-Aryan invader cultures. This produced the generally recognized schizophrenia of Greek religion, that has, on the one hand, earth-centered popular worship, and on the other, the aristocratic sky-centered "orthodox" classical religion.

Hecate is a goddess who literally straddles the earth-heaven religious divide. A member of the Olympian circle since Hesiod, her worship included the principal areas of earthly sacrality — which the Greeks called *miasma*,

206

"pollution," and her characteristic sacrifice, that of a dog, was a purification offering, that is, part of a rite meant to maintain the spiritual boundaries of the heavenly and earthly realms.

The Greeks possessed relatively few taboos (their usage defines these as ritual prohibitions relating to the state of purity in which it was permissible to approach the heavenly gods). The taboos they did have were concerned with physical uncleanness, reproduction and death. Euripides sums up the rules nicely in these lines from *Iphigeneia at Tauris*

> Any mortal stained by bloodshed,
> any mortal who has just assisted at childbirth,
> any mortal who has just touched a corpse
> is impure, must be driven away from the altar!

Hecate, a fertility goddess who by definition is deeply involved in birth and death, and who is, further, explicitly in charge of dirt and impurity, is the very embodiment of the earthy concerns that were central to indigenous Mediterranean, pre-Greek religiosity. This explains the basis of Hecate's infernalization. Introduced into the Olympian ranks by Hesiod, in spite of her now obvious unsuitability, her demonization is part of a methodical (though unconscious) attempt to reject her. Bear in mind that Cybele, Hecate's famous cognate goddess, was never admitted to Olympus. Artemis, also from Asia Minor, became a full citizen of Olympus only after transferring her inconvenient traits to Hecate.

The fertility goddesses in the Eleusis cult do not at all call into question the very deep Greek ambivalence to what fertility religion implies — the rites of Demeter and Kore are, after all, the most bracketed exception in all of Greek religion. It was literally illegal to even discuss these rites!

To add further plausibility to our theory that the demonizing of the witches and Hecate is the working out of a deep conflict between cultural strata, I will cite three outside examples of the revaluation of fertility religion as witchcraft, in all cases by nomadic, sky-god worshipping and warlike incoming populations.

The Witch of Endor, who is treated in detail above, is only a witch in the eyes of the recently arrived Hebrews — her entire practice is consistent with the norms of Canaanite agricultural religiosity.

Among the Norse, the conflict between agricultural indigenous peoples and Indo-European invaders has, in the opinion of the great scholar de Vries, left traces in accounts of the war between the two families of gods, the Vannir and the Aesir, at the start of which Gullveig (a manifestation of the Vannir fertility goddess Freya), is burnt as a witch. The Volva (prophetess) sings in *The Elder Edda*:

> She remembers the war
> — first in the world —
> when they riddled
> Gullveig with spears
> and burned her
> in the hall of Odin;
> thrice they burned her,
> the thrice born,
> often, time again;
> but yet she lives.
> They called her Heith
> in every house where she came,
> sibyl skilled in prophecy;
> she enchanted magic wands,
> she cast spells whenever she could,

she cast spells in a trance;
she was ever the joy
of evil women.

The fertility goddess of the Wampanoag Indians of Cape Cod, Squant, was originally a consort of the Creator-god Maushop, and an evident embodiment of the ocean life which sustained the tribe:

> . . . a sea woman . . . her eyes were square, her head was covered with locks of seaweed, her fingers were webbed as the tern's feet, and she sang a wild song, in which joined the Wolf-Waves who followed her, howling as they came . . . her hair was green, glistening, her body wide and flat like a ribbon of kelp . . . she was Squant, the Sea-giantess . . .

After the white man imposed his sky-inhabiting gods on the Wampanoag's earthy religion, Squant degenerated into the evil witch Granny Squannit:

> Over and over her tales are told, backward and forward like ocean combers. Medicine men of the Upper Cape say that Squannit drew her knowlege of the underness of women from her even deeper knowlege of the underness of the sea. She, as a Kelp-squaw, dragged ships down and held them below till their hulls crumbled. She, as the Water-witch, square eyed, mischievous, knew how to haunt the Gentle Giant (Maushop) till he lost remembrance of wife and children, and followed to her cave. As mer-woman with a sea-green tail, she drifted in the wake of ships, and slowed their sailing by hanging on to the keel. The captain put out the topgallants and cursed the barnacles on the hull, but the Cape sailors knew that Squant would abide unless, by chance, the mate sang the Doxology, or the moon's path cut across her trail, or star-spikes, sharp in the water, pricked her and drove her below. As a Bog-witch, she scolded the owl and the marsh-owl scolded her. She planted

quicksand on ancient trails; gathered to her breast young swamp-devils with reedy voices, and while they floated on her long black hair, she wallowed in the mud.

Only the very old Indians talk of Squant the Sea-woman; but many who live in Mashpee remember Granny Squannit as the bogey of their youth. A bad boy was certain to see her, and she was no sight for even a grown man: better keep her off by obedience and by going to sleep when told.

(The account of Granny Squannit is from Elizabeth Reynard's book *The Narrow Land*. It's worth noting that this ethnographer studied anthropology under Franz Boas at Barnard— with her friends Maya Deren and Zora Neale Hurston!)

Returning to the Greek witch, her degeneration should now appear not as a singular and cryptic phenomenon, but as the predictable outcome of a particular kind of culture-clash.

The special importance and influence of the Greek witch mythology is due to its being the crystallization and symbol of classical culture's relationship, not only to an earlier culture, but to what that culture's central goddess represented: sexually generated material existence.

One need not here tediously prove anew the weary observation that the early Greeks were uniquely responsive to the richness and charm of the physical world, which they found quite as entrancing as Odysseus' comrades did Circe in her garden among the tame wild-animals. Nor is it reasonably to be disputed that the Greeks gradually came to view the material world with the same suspicion, then dread, with which they (at the same historical point) regarded the sex-crazed hag picking magic salads in the graveyard. The fertility goddess in her descent to witch-status is a symbol of changing Greco-Roman attitudes to material existence. The late hag-like witch, with her lust and her funereal preoccupations, is an allegory of the physical appetites that bring us screaming into existence and the physical laws that send us groaning hence.

Bear in mind that the negative witch depiction, like the dark Hecate, appears only in the fifth century BC, contemporary with Plato. The same dualism which made the great philosopher and his followers see the world and sex as the doomed and rotting prison of the soul is also operant on the goddess who represents the world and sex. The witch, a late echo of the earth mother, is vilified in exactly the same terms as the material world: infernal Hecate with her torch and her cave meaningfully parallels the setting of Plato's allegoric troglodytes. The analogy with Plato's cave is even more strikingly apt when one recalls that it occurs in the exact center of Plato's *Republic*, whose setting is the feast of Bendis, a Thracian goddess with whom Hecate was conflated, and who was associated, as Hecate always was, with torches, and connected, as Hecate was (via Enodia), by the time *The Republic* was written, with horses.

Here then ends my exposition of Hecate and the witch. It only remains to add the reflection that I have not "explained away" the power and mystery of the archetype by tracing its historical phases and determinants. Hecate and the witch have had a long and fascinating life from Homer through to Shakespeare and Goethe. And judging by the films and fiction of the twentieth century, the archetype that is the witch has lost nothing of her strength.

Great symbolic images, that combine form and meaning in a unity that can be not only felt, not only understood, but both felt and understood at once, that is, experienced — these images are the points where the world of spirits has broken through into our world. To learn these is to learn the *real* rudiments of magic.

29516652R00118

Printed in Great Britain
by Amazon